Space Exploration

Book Editor

Bruce Glassman, *Vice President*
Bonnie Szumski, *Publisher*
Helen Cothran, *Managing Editor*

AT ISSUE

OPPOSING VIEWPOINTS® SERIES

GREENHAVEN PRESS
An imprint of Thomson Gale, a part of The Thomson Corporation

THOMSON
™
GALE

Detroit • New York • San Francisco • San Diego • New Haven, Conn.
Waterville, Maine • London • Munich

For more information, contact
Greenhaven Press
27500 Drake Rd.
Farmington Hills, MI 48331-3535
Or you can visit our Internet site at http://www.gale.com

LIBRARY OF CONGRESS CATALOGING-IN-PUBLICATION DATA

Space exploration / Daniel A. Leone, book editor.
    p. cm. — (At issue)
  Includes bibliographical references and index.
  ISBN 0-7377-2747-0 (lib. : alk. paper) — ISBN 0-7377-2748-9 (pbk. : alk. paper)
    1. Astronautics—Government policy—United States. [1. Outer space—
Exploration.] I. Leone, Daniel A. II. At issue (San Diego, Calif.)
  TL789.8.U5S575 2005
  333.9'4'0973—dc22
                                                                    2004058028

Printed in the United States of America

Contents

Introduction

I believe that this nation should commit itself to achieving the goal, before this decade is out, of landing a man on the Moon and returning him safely to earth.
—John F. Kennedy

In 1961 President Kennedy delivered a speech that catapulted manned space missions into the forefront of space exploration and the minds of all Americans. Although manned space flights had been planned a few years earlier, it was Kennedy who drove what would become known as the "space race" or the "race to the moon" against the Russians. Eight years later, on July 20, 1969, NASA's Apollo 11 made the first lunar landing and Neil Armstrong became the first human to step foot on another world. While this was an extraordinary accomplishment, moon flights ended in 1972. For the next three decades manned space exploration would be limited to near-Earth orbits in a new and cutting-edge spacecraft.

The space shuttle program was developed throughout the 1970s. The program's primary objective was to design a reusable spacecraft. The rocket technology used prior to the development of the space shuttle had to be rebuilt for each new launch, which became prohibitively expensive. On April 12, 1981, the space shuttle *Columbia* successfully completed the first shuttle mission. Its main goal was to test the spacecraft's systems and demonstrate a safe launch into low orbit and a safe return to Earth. Since then the space shuttle program has built six shuttles and completed many successful and scientifically valuable missions. More than one hundred documented NASA technologies from the space shuttle are now incorporated into tools, foods, and the biotechnology and medicines used to improve human health.

Although the shuttle program has demonstrated many successes and contributions to society, it also has endured some serious setbacks and criticisms. On January 28, 1986, the *Challenger* shuttle exploded shortly after takeoff, killing all seven crew members. The event caused national shock and grief, but

NASA survived and continued with its program. Seventeen years later, on February 1, 2003, the shuttle *Columbia* broke apart while reentering Earth's atmosphere, killing all seven crew members. This second disaster prompted many critics to be more vocal about the flaws and weaknesses of the space shuttle. Their primary concern was their belief that the shuttles are not safe enough. The shuttles use thirty-year-old technology and are very expensive to maintain. Critics claim that NASA, forced to operate on a tight budget, has been unable to update shuttle components with more reliable and sturdy technology. Other opponents argue that the program is obsolete and impractical for manned space flight. Originally intended to make weekly flights at a cost of $5 million per flight, current per flight costs exceed $500 million, and only four flights were scheduled in 2003. Critics also complain that the shuttle was designed too big and does not carry the payload that it was intended to. The shuttle's crash history combined with its weaknesses and inefficiencies for manned exploration have put its long-term future in doubt.

A Bold New Initiative

On January 14, 2004, President George W. Bush made a speech at NASA headquarters outlining a new and ambitious space initiative. While the president acknowledged the past success of NASA's programs, he stressed the necessity to push manned exploration beyond Earth's orbit and across the solar system.

The plan outlines three specific goals. The first goal is to complete the International Space Station by 2010. The station will be constructed in conjunction with fifteen international partners. The stated primary purpose of the station will be to provide critical research and testing of the effects of long-term space travel and exposure on humans. By using the station as a laboratory, scientists will be able to better understand and overcome the obstacles that could limit success in exploration.

The second goal is to develop and test a new spacecraft, called a Crew Exploration Vehicle, by 2008 and to complete a successful manned mission no later than 2014. The purpose of the new spacecraft project is to provide vehicles that are better suited and more cost-effective for manned space missions deep into the solar system. Consequently, upon its completion, the new spaceship program would retire the space shuttle.

The third goal is to recommence moon missions. Starting in

2008 robotic missions will research and prepare the moon for human exploration. The ultimate objective is to develop enough life-sustaining and technological equipment on the moon so that it could be used as a launch and return point for solar system exploration. The most significant expense of Earth-based launches is the rocket power needed to escape Earth's strong gravitational pull. Moon-based launches would be much more cost-effective due to the moon's much lower gravity.

The new space initiative outlined by Bush is bold and aggressive. And it also will require significant additional funding. However, as the plan covers a fifteen-year period, it will require a commitment from future presidents and government officials. It is not clear whether this commitment will materialize. What is clear is that Bush has laid out a challenge and a new vision for manned space exploration that has inspired many Americans.

Supporters of the space initiative believe that it will reignite global interest in manned space exploration of the solar system and perhaps beyond. Some believe that colonization of other worlds is the ultimate solution to chronic problems that threaten Earth's future, such as pollution, overpopulation, shrinking resources, global warming, and asteroid collisions. They claim that mankind can survive and flourish by not relying solely on a fragile and vulnerable Earth. They state that exploration of the solar system cannot only provide resources to solve many of Earth's problems but can yield new living environments as well. As stated by the famous futurist Arthur C. Clarke, "Many, and some of the most pressing, of our terrestrial problems can be solved only by going into space. Long before it was a vanishing commodity, the wilderness as the preservation of the world was proclaimed by [nineteenth-century American writer Henry David] Thoreau. In the new wilderness of the Solar System may lie the future preservation of mankind."

Buzz Aldrin, the second man to walk on the moon, also believes strongly that mankind's future will be in the colonization of space and other worlds. As he stated in a *Los Angeles Times* column,

> We have to start thinking seriously about the notion of public space travel and commercial activity in space. Beginning with government research and exploration, we need to move towards private citizens in space. We must develop mature rockets and spacecraft as well as hotels and habitats in low

orbit for public space travel. From that base we can
venture beyond low orbit to the moon, to asteroids and to Mars.

Others add that in addition to the benefits to mankind of space
colonization, investments in space reap dividends on Earth by
creating jobs, economic activity, and technological and scientific innovations.

While many support the space initiative and a bolder plan
for manned space exploration, others oppose such massive investments in space. Some argue that unmanned exploration has
proven much more cost-effective than manned missions while
yielding significant results. They claim that the majority of scientific discoveries have come from unmanned probes, telescopes, and satellites. These devices have cost a fraction of what
NASA has spent to develop and maintain its manned space
program. Paul Krugman, an economics professor at Princeton
University and a columnist for the *New York Times*, explains,
"Manned space travel will remain prohibitively expensive until
there is a breakthrough in propulsion and even then will there
be any reason to send people, rather than our ever more sophisticated machines, into space?"

Other critics of the new space initiative complain that
while hundreds of billions of dollars have been spent on space
exploration, billions of people continue to suffer on Earth.
They argue that while space is interesting and alluring, there
are real problems to solve on Earth such as disease, hunger,
poverty, and illiteracy. Until these problems are resolved, they
believe that any available resources for unessential programs
such as space exploration should be redirected to improve people's lives on Earth.

Humankind has pondered the heavens for thousands of
years. For over thirty years, humans have been active in space.
At Issue: Space Exploration explores the debates over manned exploration and the colonization of space as well as other issues,
such as the search for extraterrestrial life and whether weapons
should be in space.

1

The United States Must Make Space Exploration a Priority

George W. Bush

George W. Bush is the president of the United States.

Although the U.S. space program has been successful and productive over the past decades, much exploration and discovery remains to be done. It has been thirty years since a human being has set foot on the moon. It is important that mankind continue to explore the solar system and beyond. To provide a platform for this exploration, it is imperative that the International Space Station be completed, a new spacecraft program be developed, and manned trips to the moon recommence. These important steps will yield crucial research about the long-term effects of living in space as well as allow for more efficient and cost effective space travel.

America is proud of our space program. The risk takers and visionaries of this agency have expanded human knowledge, have revolutionized our understanding of the universe, and produced technological advances that have benefited all of humanity.

Inspired by all that has come before, and guided by clear objectives, today we set a new course for America's space program. We will give NASA a new focus and vision for future exploration. We will build new ships to carry man forward into the universe, to gain a new foothold on the moon, and to prepare for new journeys to worlds beyond our own. . . .

George W. Bush, speech at NASA Headquarters, Washington, DC, January 14, 2004.

The Benefits of Space Exploration

Two centuries ago, Meriwether Lewis and William Clark left St. Louis to explore the new lands acquired in the Louisiana Purchase. They made that journey in the spirit of discovery, to learn the potential of vast new territory, and to chart a way for others to follow.

America has ventured forth into space for the same reasons. We have undertaken space travel because the desire to explore and understand is part of our character. And that quest has brought tangible benefits that improve our lives in countless ways. The exploration of space has led to advances in weather forecasting, in communications, in computing, search and rescue technology, robotics, and electronics. Our investment in space exploration helped to create our satellite telecommunications network and the Global Positioning System. Medical technologies that help prolong life—such as the imaging processing used in CAT scanners and MRI machines—trace their origins to technology engineered for the use in space.

> *We have undertaken space travel because the desire to explore and understand is part of our character.*

Our current programs and vehicles for exploring space have brought us far and they have served us well. The space shuttle has flown more than a hundred missions. It has been used to conduct important research and to increase the sum of human knowledge. Shuttle crews, and the scientists and engineers who support them, have helped to build the International Space Station.

Telescopes—including those in space—have revealed more than 100 planets in the last decade alone. Probes have shown us stunning images of the rings of Saturn and the outer planets of our solar system. Robotic explorers have found evidence of water—a key ingredient for life—on Mars and on the moons of Jupiter. At this very hour, the Mars Exploration Rover Spirit is searching for evidence of life beyond the Earth.

Yet for all these successes, much remains for us to explore and to learn. In the past 30 years, no human being has set foot on another world, or ventured farther upward into space than

386 miles—roughly the distance from Washington, D.C., to Boston, Massachusetts. America has not developed a new vehicle to advance human exploration in space in nearly a quarter century. It is time for America to take the next steps.

A New Plan to Explore Space

Today I announce a new plan to explore space and extend a human presence across our solar system. We will begin the effort quickly, using existing programs and personnel. We'll make steady progress—one mission, one voyage, one landing at a time.

Our first goal is to complete the International Space Station by 2010. We will finish what we have started, we will meet our obligations to our 15 international partners on this project. We will focus our future research aboard the station on the long-term effects of space travel on human biology. The environment of space is hostile to human beings. Radiation and weightlessness pose dangers to human health, and we have much to learn about their long-term effects before human crews can venture through the vast voids of space for months at a time. Research on board the station and here on Earth will help us better understand and overcome the obstacles that limit exploration. Through these efforts we will develop the skills and techniques necessary to sustain further space exploration.

> *Our first goal is to complete the International Space Station by 2010.*

To meet this goal, we will return the space shuttle to flight as soon as possible, consistent with safety concerns and the recommendations of the Columbia Accident Investigation Board.[1] The shuttle's chief purpose over the next several years will be to help finish assembly of the International Space Station. In 2010, the space shuttle—after nearly 30 years of duty—will be retired from service.

Our second goal is to develop and test a new spacecraft, the

---

1. On February 1, 2003, the space shuttle *Columbia* broke apart while reentering the atmosphere, killing all seven crew members.

Crew Exploration Vehicle, by 2008, and to conduct the first manned mission no later than 2014. The Crew Exploration Vehicle will be capable of ferrying astronauts and scientists to the Space Station after the shuttle is retired. But the main purpose of this spacecraft will be to carry astronauts beyond our orbit to other worlds. This will be the first spacecraft of its kind since the Apollo Command Module.

Our third goal is to return to the moon by 2020, as the launching point for missions beyond. Beginning no later than 2008, we will send a series of robotic missions to the lunar surface to research and prepare for future human exploration. Using the Crew Exploration Vehicle, we will undertake extended human missions to the moon as early as 2015, with the goal of living and working there for increasingly extended periods. Eugene Cernan, who is with us today—the last man to set foot on the lunar surface—said this as he left: "We leave as we came, and God willing as we shall return, with peace and hope for all mankind." America will make those words come true.

> *Our third goal is to return to the moon by 2020.*

Returning to the moon is an important step for our space program. Establishing an extended human presence on the moon could vastly reduce the costs of further space exploration, making possible ever more ambitious missions. Lifting heavy space craft and fuel out of the Earth's gravity is expensive. Spacecraft assembled and provisioned on the moon could escape its far lower gravity using far less energy, and thus, far less cost. Also, the moon is home to abundant resources. Its soil contains raw materials that might be harvested and processed into rocket fuel or breathable air. We can use our time on the moon to develop and test new approaches and technologies and systems that will allow us to function in other, more challenging environments. The moon is a logical step toward further progress and achievement.

With the experience and knowledge gained on the moon, we will then be ready to take the next steps of space exploration: human missions to Mars and to worlds beyond. Robotic missions will serve as trailblazers—the advanced guard to the unknown. Probes, landers and other vehicles of this kind continue to prove their worth, sending spectacular images and vast amounts of data back to Earth. Yet the human thirst for knowledge ultimately cannot be satisfied by even the most vivid pictures, or the most detailed measurements. We need to see and examine and touch for ourselves. And only human beings are capable of adapting to the inevitable uncertainties posed by space travel.

Headed into the Cosmos

As our knowledge improves, we'll develop new power generation, propulsion, life support, and other systems that can support more distant travels. We do not know where this journey will end, yet we know this: human beings are headed into the cosmos.

And along this journey we'll make many technological breakthroughs. We don't know yet what those breakthroughs will be, but we can be certain they'll come, and that our efforts will be repaid many times over. We may discover resources on the moon or Mars that will boggle the imagination, that will test our limits to dream. And the fascination generated by further exploration will inspire our young people to study math, and science, and engineering and create a new generation of innovators and pioneers.

This will be a great and unifying mission for NASA, and we know that you'll achieve it. I have directed Administrator O'Keefe to review all of NASA's current space flight and exploration activities and direct them toward the goals I have outlined. I will also form a commission of private and public sector experts to advise on implementing the vision that I've outlined today. This commission will report to me within four months of its first meeting. I'm today naming former Secretary of the Air Force, Pete Aldridge, to be the Chair of the Commission. Thank you for being here today, Pete. He has tremendous experience in the Department of Defense and the aerospace industry. He is going to begin this important work right away.

We'll invite other nations to share the challenges and opportunities of this new era of discovery. The vision I outline today is a journey, not a race, and I call on other nations to join us on this journey, in a spirit of cooperation and friendship.

Achieving these goals requires a long-term commitment. NASA's current five-year budget is $86 billion. Most of the funding we need for the new endeavors will come from reallocating $11 billion within that budget. We need some new resources, however. I will call upon Congress to increase NASA's budget by roughly a billion dollars, spread out over the next five years. This increase, along with refocusing of our space agency, is a solid beginning to meet the challenges and the goals we set today. It's only a beginning. Future funding decisions will be guided by the progress we make in achieving our goals.

We begin this venture knowing that space travel brings great risks. The loss of the space shuttle *Columbia* was less than one year ago. Since the beginning of our space program, America has lost 23 astronauts, and one astronaut from an allied nation—men and women who believed in their mission and accepted the dangers. As one family member said, "The legacy of *Columbia* must carry on—for the benefit of our children and yours." The *Columbia*'s crew did not turn away from the challenge, and neither will we.

Mankind is drawn to the heavens for the same reason we were once drawn into unknown lands and across the open sea. We choose to explore space because doing so improves our lives, and lifts our national spirit. So let us continue the journey.

May God bless.

2

The Government's Space Plan Has Merit

Austin American-Statesman

The Austin American-Statesman *is a daily newspaper in Austin, Texas.*

The government's new space plan, with the ultimate goal of manned exploration of Mars, raises concerns about costs. However, the proposal should not be judged on this basis alone. Any analysis of the plan should include the many potential economic and technological benefits of space exploration. NASA's presence in Texas directly and indirectly has created thousands of jobs and billions of dollars in economic activity and has pushed the state into a technologically based economy. Additionally, the reinvigorated space program will redirect and reorganize NASA as it pursues a bold new goal of exploration. The effect will not be unlike the one created by President Kennedy over forty years ago in his race to reach the moon.

Concerns raised about the cost of a reinvigorated space program as proposed by President Bush should not be used as an excuse to dismiss his ideas without a fair hearing. Moreover, that hearing should take into account the economic and technological potential of the Mars undertaking, not just the cost of getting there.

It's an election year [2004], though, and imploring politicians to be intellectually honest is like asking a shark not to eat. Besides the discussion of cost, there will be talk of the hazard. Being cognizant of danger is one thing; surrendering to it is quite another. Had Queen Isabella surrendered to cost concerns, Columbus never would have left Spain. Had the Wright brothers given in to fear, they would have remained just another couple of bicycle mechanics from Ohio.

Yes, exploration of space by humans is dangerous and expensive. As President Kennedy noted in a speech at Rice University in Houston in 1962: "We choose to go to the moon in this decade, and do the other things—not because they are easy; but because they are hard; because that goal will serve to organize and measure the best of our energies and skills; because that challenge is one that we're willing to accept; one we are unwilling to postpone, and one we intend to win. . . ."

> *Being cognizant of danger is one thing; surrendering to it is quite another.*

Bush has taken up the challenge his predecessor laid down 42 years ago. The National Aeronautics and Space Administration, for all the good work that it has done in the time since Camelot,[1] is long overdue for reorganization and redirection. When Bush outlined his idea of manned exploration of Mars by 2030, NASA officials got the message: Change is coming.

Actually, it couldn't come at a better time. In many ways, NASA is a victim of its own success. So blase are we about space travel that we are shocked when something goes wrong, as it did with the two shuttle flights that ended in tragedy, in 1986 and 2003.[2]

The Space Program's Economic Potential

There are a lot of good reasons to proceed cautiously with such a big expense, and examining the president's proposal with a critical eye will no doubt strengthen it. An honest study, however, will also calculate the economic potential of such an undertaking.

When Kennedy delivered those remarks in Houston, it was

1. The time of John F. Kennedy's presidency is sometimes referred to as "Camelot."   2. In 1986 the space shuttle *Challenger* exploded on takeoff, killing all seven crewmembers. In 2003 the shuttle *Columbia* broke apart while reentering the earth's atmosphere, killing all seven on board.

an entirely different city in an entirely different state. Rich Texans were a caricature, poor ones were the reality. Space exploration filled imaginations and wallets.

The economic stimulus of the space program obviously benefited Houston, but its impact on the state is incalculable. According to figures compiled by the Bay Area Houston Economic Partnership, the Johnson Space Center accounts for 16,251 jobs in the Houston area. Those jobs translate to more than $885 million in business volume, and personal incomes of more than $2 billion. The space center is responsible for more than 49,000 jobs in Texas, which produce $2.2 billion in business volume and $4.2 billion in personal income.

There is no doubt that NASA's presence in Texas made possible the state's move toward a technological economy. While that economy is not immune to downturn, there is no turning back, despite the yearnings of ardent nostalgia lovers.

Obviously, a lot has changed since JFK delivered those words in Houston. We do not, for example, have the Cold War to lend an urgency to capturing the ultimate high ground. But the most basic reason for reaching into space hasn't changed.

In that Houston speech, Kennedy replied to critics who questioned his vision for exploring space: "But why, some say, the moon? Why choose this as our goal? And they may well ask why climb the highest mountain? Why 35 years ago fly the Atlantic? Why does Rice play Texas?"

Why, indeed.

3

The Government's Space Plan Is Flawed

Denver Post

The Denver Post *is a daily newspaper in Denver, Colorado.*

The government's new space plan has outlined a broad goal of manned Mars exploration but neglects to explain how the significant costs will be supported. To fund such an ambitious plan, domestic programs will have to be cut and NASA will have to eliminate many of its less glamorous yet productive projects. Although NASA has been criticized for not moving farther into space for the past three decades, the truth is that the most significant benefits of space exploration have been realized closer to home. While there may be some real economic and technological benefits of returning to the moon in a few decades, the costs of manned missions to Mars at this point far outweigh the benefits.

President Bush's plan to send humans back to the moon and on to Mars is more political fiction than science. Bush outlined a broad goal but neglected details like how to pay for it. Moreover, a human Mars mission may not be the best way to gain scientific insights.

Certainly, humans should explore the solar system, but the effort must have do-able budgets, realistic prospects for developing the necessary technologies and clear scientific or security aims. The Bush plan lacks all those elements.

Instead, Bush's announcement smacks of political grandstanding. It got the public talking, at least temporarily, more about Mars than about Iraq or the deficit, but talk can be short-lived.

Bush essentially embraced an updated version of a Mars plan that his dad, the first President Bush, proposed in 1989 but couldn't get off the ground. The reasons the first plan went nowhere still exist: Sending people to Mars would cost too much, divert NASA from more useful work and accomplish nothing that couldn't be done at less cost by unmanned vehicles.

The Wrong Direction

Focusing money on Mars won't take the space program in the right direction.

By abandoning the already scaled-down international space station less than a decade after its completion, Bush will have trashed a multibillion-dollar investment without giving it a chance to produce scientific or economic benefits. He also will have found a new way to annoy 15 allied countries involved in the station.

> *Focusing money on Mars won't take the space program in the right direction.*

The next question is how to fund a Mars project that may cost a half-trillion dollars. The answer: By slashing domestic programs and gutting NASA's other important, if less glamorous, work.

NASA needs at least another $1 billion over the next five years on top of its existing $86 billion budget to come close to Bush's goal. It also will have to take $11 billion out of its own hide by ending other programs. What does Bush want to discard? Global climate studies? The Hubble telescope's replacement?

Are there better ways to explore space in the near term? Yes. NASA has been criticized for going in circles for three decades, but in truth most benefits of space exploration have come from close-to-home missions. Global communications, better air and ship navigation and more accurate weather prediction all stemmed from work first done by NASA. It's possible to envision real scientific and economic benefits by returning to the moon in a few decades—but not, at this point, for putting humans on Mars.

One part of Bush's plan does make sense: Retire the space shuttle and replace it with a less costly but more reliable craft. However, that project already was on the drawing board.

After the shuttle *Columbia* disintegrated last year [2003], a blue-ribbon panel ripped NASA for lacking a vision of its future. By putting Mars on the agenda, Bush and NASA chief Sean O'Keefe may hope to give the agency that vision. But a vision that ignores practical concerns is just a fantasy.

4

Space Exploration Provides Many Benefits for Earth

David J. Eicher

David J. Eicher is the editor of Astronomy *magazine. He is the author of seven books on astronomy and has a minor planet, 3617 Eicher, named for him.*

Cell phones, MRIs, DVDs, and smoke detectors are just a few of the technological advances that are attributable to NASA and its research. While many believe the $15 billion space budget could be put to better use on earth, they fail to acknowledge all the dividends that this investment has paid to society and its standard of living. As NASA begins to push its goals to the moon, Mars, and beyond, it will simultaneously push technology and innovation to new heights. Even those unimpressed with space exploration will eventually benefit from everyday advances borne from NASA research that will more than justify any increases in the space budget. The farther NASA reaches into space, the more society on earth will benefit.

The next time you reach for your cellphone, thank NASA. If your doctor recommends an MRI, thank NASA. The space agency deserves another moment of gratitude when you pop in a DVD and settle back for a good movie, or when you reach for a composite golf club, hoping to out-drive your buddies. And think of NASA when a smoke detector blares to save your life.

NASA often is relegated to elitist-bureaucracy status, seen as

David J. Eicher, "Despite Far-Reaching Goals, NASA Benefits Earth Most," *USA Today*, January 22, 2004. Copyright © 2004 by *USA Today*. Reproduced by permission of the author.

driven by starry-eyed scientists looking to grab funds away from better use on Earth. But since the days of Apollo, NASA has contributed to the technological advancement of everyday life on Earth as much as—and maybe more than—anything else. That's why President [George W.] Bush's new space initiative, while expensive, will pay back incalculable dividends to everyone on Earth during the coming decades, just as the Apollo program did.

> *The next time you reach for your cellphone, thank NASA.*

Bush and NASA Administrator Sean O'Keefe contend that "seed money" of $1 billion during the next five years will initiate this bold new move, which includes a return to the moon by about 2015, construction of a lunar base five years later and a manned mission to Mars by about 2030.

They suggest the bulk of this money will come from shifting priorities within NASA's budget, now $15.5 billion annually. Indeed, the price will be high in both cost and priorities; the Hubble Space Telescope, for example, will be doomed because it no longer will be serviced after the musty and unreliable fleet of space shuttles is relegated to the Smithsonian.

Windfall for Astronomy

But the shock waves emanating from a change from low-Earth orbit, with its limited scientific value, to deep-space exploration will rock the science world. Much of what will follow could be done robotically and—in the short term—for a lower cost. Ultimately, however, what must be done on the moon and on Mars can be done only with a human on site, making the immediate decisions that a computer cannot.

Astronomers and planetary scientists will experience a windfall if the Bush initiative receives congressional blessing. What humans learn about the moon and the Red Planet will put the big questions of the rarity of life in the universe into stark perspective and will tell us much about Earth's own future, the fate of the solar system and our cosmic genesis.

Humans stand on the threshold of answering these questions: how the universe formed, how we came to be and where it is all going. That kind of explorative curiosity—"to see what's over the next hill," as O'Keefe puts it—is, after all, the most important thing that separates humans from Douglas firs.

Even those without a passion for exploration will see big gains right here on the home planet as engineers push technology and innovation forward. New exploration vehicles will spur changes in aircraft travel on Earth. Education will get the spark it so desperately needs as space exploration once again fires the imaginations of millions of children. Most of the gains, however, will be at the everyday-life level. The money will be used to employ thousands and push technology to unknowable heights.

Forty years ago, NASA engineers didn't start one Monday morning by saying, "Gee, I think I'll work on microchip technology that, 30 years downstream, will lead to digital cameras." But that's what happened. The technological gains that come out of research arise from a kind of ripple effect: advance on top of advance, technology growing out of technology.

Those who control NASA's budget cannot predict the most exciting things that will change the way we live our lives a generation hence. But they will find new technology, and Americans will use it, just as we now use GPS receivers, ski jackets and plastic bags for our leftovers. Even those unmoved by human exploration will see everyday advances well worth NASA's new budget.

Regrettably, Bush did not further outline his plans in [his 2004] State of the Union address. We will need to wait to understand the initiative's details. But one thing already is clear. If his plans become reality, the moon and Mars will be new worlds—and so will Earth.

5

Space Exploration Should Focus on Mars and the Colonization of Other Worlds

Charles Krauthammer

Charles Krauthammer is a syndicated columnist whose work appears in the Washington Post *and* Time. *He is a contributing editor to the* Weekly Standard.

America has lost interest and its will for space exploration. It has been over thirty years since a human being has been to the moon. In that time, the majority of the space budget has been spent on the space shuttle circling the earth in low orbit conducting environmental experiments and other earth-related research. The nation needs to reinvigorate its passion to explore the heavens. This effort must begin with more generous funding to support a modern program for unmanned and manned space travel to the moon and Mars. There is new evidence that water exists on both surfaces. This would make manned space missions much more practical and cost effective as the water could be used to make life-sustaining oxygen as well as hydrogen for fuel for return trips. America has waited long enough and has no legitimate excuses not to resume its exploration of space and perhaps one day colonize other worlds.

What manner of creature are we? It took 100,000 years for humans to get inches off the ground. Then, astonishingly, it took only 66 to get from Kitty Hawk to the moon. And then, still more astonishingly, we lost interest, spending the remaining 30 years of the 20th century going around in circles in low earth orbit, i.e., going nowhere.

[In July 1999], the unmanned Lunar Prospector probe was sent to find out whether the moon contains water. It was a remarkable venture, but even more remarkable was the fact that Prospector was the first NASA spacecraft, manned or unmanned, to land on the moon since the last Apollo astronaut departed in 1972. Twenty-seven years without even a glance back.

We remember the late 15th and 16th centuries as the Age of Exploration. The second half of the 20th was at one point known as the Space Age. What happened? For the first 20 years we saw space as a testing ground, an arena for splendid, strenuous exertion. We were in a race with the Soviets for space supremacy, and mobilized for it as for war. President Kennedy committed all of our resources: men, materiel, money, and spirit. And he was bold. When he promised to land a man on the moon before the decade was out, there were only eight and a half years left. At the time, no American had even orbited the earth.

The Apollo program was a triumph. But the public quickly grew bored. The interview with the moon-bound astronauts aboard *Apollo 13* was not even broadcast, for lack of an audience. It was only when the flight turned into a harrowing drama of survival that an audience assembled. By *Apollo 17*, it was all over. The final three moonshots were canceled for lack of interest.

The Shuttle: A Dead End

Looking to reinvent itself, NASA came up with the idea of a space shuttle ferrying men and machines between earth and an orbiting space station. It was a fine idea except for one thing: There was no space station. *Skylab* had been launched in May 1973, then manned for 171 days. But no effort was made to keep its orbit from decaying. It fell to earth and burned. We were left with an enormously expensive shuttle—to nowhere.

The shuttle has had its successes—the views of earth it brought back, the repairs to the Hubble space telescope it enabled. But it has been a dead end scientifically and deadening spiritually. There is today a palpable ennui with space. When did we last get excited? When a 77-year-old man climbed into the shuttle in November 1998 for a return flight. That was the most excitement the shuttle program had engendered in years—the first time in a long time that a launch and the preparations and even the preflight press conference had received live coverage. Televisions were hauled into classrooms so kids could watch.

But watch what? The fact is that we were watching John Glenn reprise a flight he'd made 36 years earlier. It is as if the Wright Brothers had returned to Kitty Hawk in 1939 to skim the sand once again, and the replay was treated as some great advance in aviation.

> *// The second half of the 20th [century] was at one point known as the Space Age. //*

The most disturbing part of the Glenn phenomenon was the efflorescence of space nostalgia—at a time when space exploration is still in its infancy. We have not really gone anywhere yet, and we are already looking back with sweet self-satisfaction.

The other flutter of excitement generated by the shuttle program occurred a few years earlier when Shannon Lucid received the Congressional Space Medal of Honor for a long-duration flight in low earth orbit. A sign of the times. She is surely brave and spunky, but the lavish attention her feat garnered says much about the diminished state of our space program. Endurance records are fine. But the Congressional Space Medal of Honor? It used to be given to the likes of Alan Shepard and John Glenn, who had the insane courage to park themselves atop an unstable, spanking-new, largely untested eight-story bomb not knowing whether it would blow up under them. Now we give it for spending six months in an orbiting phone booth with a couple of guys named Yuri.

An Inward-Turning Time

What happened? Where is the national will to explore? We are stuck along some quiet historical sidetrack. The fascination today is with communication, calculation, miniaturization, all in the service of multiplying human interconnectedness. Outer space has ceded pride of place to the inner space of the Internet. In fact, space's greatest claim on our interest and resources currently rests on the fact that satellites allow us to page each other and confirm that 9:30 meeting about the new Tostitos ad campaign.

The excitement surrounding Shannon Lucid's six months of sponge baths and Russian food aboard *Mir* is a reflection of the quiet domesticity of this inward-turning time. Perhaps it is the exhaustion after 60 years of world war, cold and hot, stretching right up to the early 1990s. The *Seinfeld* era is not an era for Odyssean adventures. Now is a time for home and hearth—the glowing computer screen that allows endless intercourse with our fellow humans.

Another reason for the diminishing drive for planetary exploration is, perversely, the fruits of the moon landing itself—and in particular that famous photograph of earth taken by the Apollo astronauts during the first human circumnavigation of another celestial body.

"Earthrise" had an important effect on human consciousness. It gave us our first view of earth as it is seen from God's perspective: warm, safe, serene, blessed. It created a kind of pre-emptive nostalgia for earth, at precisely the moment when earthlings were finally acquiring the ability to leave it.

It is no surprise that "Earthrise" should have become such a cultural icon, particularly for the environmental Left. It offered the cosmic equivalent of the call to "Come home, America" issued just four years after the picture was taken.

That photo and the ethos it promoted—global, sedentary, inward-looking—were the metaphysical complement to the political arguments made at the time, and ever since, for turning our gaze from space back to earth. These are the familiar arguments about social priorities: Why are we spending all this money on space, when there is poverty and disease and suffering at home?

Missing the Point

It is a maddening question because, while often offered in good faith, it entirely misses the point. Poverty and disease will always be with us. We have spent, by most estimates, some $5 trillion trying to abolish poverty in the United States alone. Government is simply not very good at solving social problems. But it can be extremely good at solving technical problems. The Manhattan Project is, of course, the classic case. As are the various technological advances forged in war, from radar to computers.

Concerted national mobilization for a specific scientific

objective can have great success. This is in sharp contrast to national mobilization for social objectives, which almost invariably ends in disappointment, waste, and unintended consequences (such as the dependency and deviancy spawned by the massive welfare programs and entitlements of the sixties and the seventies—the Left's preferred destination for the resources supposedly squandered on space).

> **"** *Where is the national will to explore?* **"**

But more exasperating than the poor social science and the misapprehension about the real capacities of government is the tone-deafness of the earth-firsters to the wonder and glory of space, and to the unique opportunity offered this generation. How can one live at the turn of the 21st century, when the planets are for the first time within our grasp, and not be moved by the grandeur of the enterprise?

NASA administrators like to talk about science and spinoffs to justify the space program. Well, the study of bone decalcification in near-earth weightlessness is fine, but it is hardly the motor force behind President Kennedy's ringing declaration, "We choose to go to the Moon." That is not why we, as a people and as a species, ventured into the cosmos in the first place.

Teflon and pagers are nice, too, and perhaps effective politically in selling space. But they are hardly the point. We are going into space for the same reason George Mallory climbed Everest: Because it is there. For the adventure, for the romance, for the sheer temerity of venturing into the void.

Contracting Our Horizons

And yet, amid the national psychic letdown that followed the moon landings and is still with us today, that kind of talk seems archaic, anachronistic. So what do we do? We radically contract our horizons. We spend three decades tumbling about in near-earth orbit. We become expert in zero-G nausea and other fascinations. And when we do venture out into the glorious void, we do it on the very cheap, to accommodate the diminished national will and the pinched national resources allocated for exploration.

The reason NASA administrator Daniel Goldin adopted the "faster, better, cheaper" approach is that he was forced to. He was rightly afraid that when you send a $1 billion probe loaded with experiments and hardware and it fails (as happened to the Mars Observer in 1993), you risk losing your entire congressional backing—and your entire program. He had little choice but to adopt a strategy of sending cheaper but more vulnerable probes in order to lessen the stakes riding on each launch. Probes like the Mars Polar Lander.

When the Mars Polar Lander disappeared [in January 2000], the country went into a snit. The public felt let down, cheated of the exotic entertainment NASA was supposed to deliver. The press was peeved, deprived of a nice big story with lovely pictures. Jay Leno, the nation's leading political indicator, was merciless. ("If you're stuck for something to get NASA for Christmas, you can't go wrong with a subscription to *Popular Mechanics*. . . . But they're not giving up. NASA said they're gonna continue to look for other forms of intelligent life in the universe. And when they find it, they're gonna hire him.") And Congress preened, displaying concern, pulling its chin and promising hearings on the failure of the last three Mars missions. This will be a bit of Kabuki theater in which clueless politicians, whose greatest mathematical feat is calculating last week's fund-raising take, will pinion earnest scientists about why they could not land a go-cart on the South Pole of a body 400 million miles away on a part of the planet we had never explored.

In other words, we are in for a spell of national bellyaching and finger-pointing which will inevitably culminate in the crucifixion of a couple of NASA administrators, a few symbolic budget cuts, and a feeling of self-satisfaction all around.

The biggest scandal of the Mars exploration projects is not that a few have failed, but the way the nation has reacted to those failures. A people couched and ready, expectant and entitled, armed with a remote control yet denied Martian pictures to go with their *Today* show coffee, will be avenged.

Who is to blame for the Mars disasters? Not the scientists, but the people who will soon be putting them on trial.

Lack of Will, Laughable Budgets

Landing on another planet is very hard. And landing on its South Pole, terra incognita for us, is even harder. As one researcher put it, this *is* rocket science. "Look at the history of landers on Mars," professor Howard McCurdy of American University told the *Washington Post.* "Of twelve attempts, three have made it. The Soviets lost all six of theirs. . . . Mars really eats spacecraft."

Something this hard requires not just technology—which we have—but will, which we don't. And national will is expressed in funding. Since the glory days of Apollo, space exploration has progressively been starved. Today, funding for NASA is one fifth what it was in 1965, less than 0.8 percent of the federal budget.

And not only has the overall NASA budget declined, but so has the fraction allocated to both manned and unmanned exploration of the moon and the planets. The budget has been eaten by the space shuttle and the low-earth-orbit space station being built two decades late to finally provide a destination for the wandering shuttle.

> *The whole idea of space exploration was to find out what is out* there.

Then there is what NASA calls "mission to planet earth," a program devoted to studying such terrestrial concerns as ozone, land use, climate variability, and such. A nice idea. But it used to be NASA's mission to lift us above ozone and land and climate to reach for something higher. The whole idea of space exploration was to find out what is out *there.*

The cost of the Mars Polar Lander was $165 million. In an $8 trillion economy, that is a laughable sum. [The 1995 movie] *Waterworld* cost more. The new Bellagio hotel in Vegas could buy eight Polar Landers with $80 million left over for a bit of gambling. To put it in terms of competing space outlays, $165 million is less than half the cost of a shuttle launch. For the price of a single shuttle mission (launch, flight time, landing, and overhead) we could have sent two Mars Polar Landers and gotten $70 million back in change.

Planetary exploration is so hamstrung financially that the Polar Lander—which NASA officially declared dead—sent no telemetry during its final descent onto the planet. That was to save money. We'll never know what went wrong. Adding a black box, something to send simple signals to tell us what happened, would have cost $5 million. Five million! That doesn't buy one minute of air time on the Super Bowl.

> **"** *It is not as if we have nowhere to go but endlessly around earth.* **"**

The hard fact is that the kind of cheap, fast spacecraft NASA has been forced to build does reduce the loss in case of failure. But it increases the chance of failure. You cannot build in the kind of backup systems that go into the larger craft we sent exploring in the past. The Viking missions that 25 years ago touched down on Mars and gave us those extraordinary first pictures of its surface, and the Voyager spacecraft that gave us magnificent flybys of the entire solar system, typically cost 10 to 20 times more than the new "faster, better, cheaper" projects.

It is a travesty that the very same Congress that has squeezed funding for these programs will now be conducting the inquisition to find out why this shoestring operation could not produce another spectacular success. But we can't just blame the politicians. This is a democracy. They are responding to their constituency. Their constituency is disappointed that it received no entertainment from the Mars Polar Lander, for which the average American contributed the equivalent of half a cheeseburger. If we had had the will to devote a whole cheeseburger to a Mars lander, it could have been equipped with redundant systems, and might have succeeded.

To the Moon and Mars

The fault, dear Brutus, is not in our stars, but in ourselves. What then to do? If we are going to save resources in acknowledgment of the diminished national will to explore, we should begin by shutting the maw that is swallowing up so much of the space budget: the shuttle and the space station. It is not as if we have nowhere to go but endlessly around earth. Recent discoveries have given us new ways and new reasons for establishing a human presence on the moon and on Mars.

Until a few years ago, it could have been argued that a moon base was impractical, and human Mars exploration even more so. But there is evidence that there may be water on the moon (in the form of ice, of course). And water, there as here, is the key to everything. It could provide both life support and fuel. Similarly, the fact that there is ice on Mars has led to a revolution in thinking about how we can travel there and back. Instead of carrying huge stores of fuel, which would make the launch vehicle enormously expensive and cumbersome, we could send unmanned spacecraft ahead. They would land on Mars and turn the water into life support and fuel. (If you split water, you get hydrogen and oxygen, precisely the gases that you need for life and for propulsion.) Astronauts could travel fairly light, arriving at a place already prepared with life-sustaining water, oxygen, and hydrogen for the flight back.

> *The moon and Mars are beckoning.*

The moon and Mars are beckoning. So why are we spending so much of our resources building a tinker-toy space station? In part because, a quarter-century late, we still need something to justify the shuttle. Yet the space station's purpose has shrunk to almost nothing. No one takes seriously its claims to be a platform for real science. And the original idea—hatched in the 1950s—that it would be a way station to the moon and Mars, was overtaken in the sixties when we found more efficient ways to fully escape earth's gravitational well.

The space station's main purpose now appears to be . . . fostering international cooperation. It became too expensive for the United States to do alone, and so we decided to share the cost and control. It provides a convenient back door for American funding of the bankrupt Russian space program. We send Russia the money to build its space station modules. This is supposed to promote friendship and keep Russian rocket scientists from moving to Baghdad.

The cost to the United States? Twenty-one billion dollars, enough to support 127 Polar Landers. Instead of squandering $21 billion on a weightless United Nations (don't we have one of these already?), we should be directing our resources at the next logical step: a moon base. It would be a magnificent platform for science, for observation of the universe, and for industry. It would also be good training for Mars. And it would begin the ultimate adventure: the colonization of other worlds.

In 1991, the Stafford Commission recommended the establishment of permanent human outposts on the moon and on Mars by the early decades of this century. Rather than frittering away billions on the space station, we should be going right now to the moon—where we've been, where we know how to go, and where we might very well discover life-sustaining materials. And from there, on to the planets.

In the end, we will surely go. But how long will it take? Five hundred years from now—a time as distant from us as is Columbus—a party of settlers on excursion to Mars's South Pole will stumble across some strange wreckage, just as today we stumble across the wreckage of long-forgotten ships caught in Arctic ice. They'll wonder what manner of creature it was that sent it. What will we have told them? That after millennia of gazing at the heavens, we took one step into the void, then turned and, for the longest time, retreated to home and hearth? Or that we retained our nerve and hunger for horizons, and embraced our destiny?

6

The United States Should Militarize and Dominate Space

John J. Miller

John J. Miller is a national political reporter for National Review, *a conservative weekly magazine.*

The U.S. military has had a presence in space for years with its arsenal of satellite and communication systems orbiting earth. However, while this technology provides critical guidance for ground and air operations, it does not provide security against offensive missile strikes directed at the United States. The military domination of space will be essential to national security in the twenty-first century. Opponents of space weapons argue that their presence will cause a dangerous space race and threaten global stability. Yet military domination of space can actually have a stabilizing effect across the globe. With a supreme, space-based, antiballistic missile laser system covering the globe, the United States would create a lasting deterrent against offensive missile strikes against any nation. Long-standing conflicts between nations with nuclear capabilities, such as India and Pakistan, could be controlled and checked without taking sides. By controlling space, America could create a safe space environment, fostering commerce and scientific research while also reserving the ability to act against any threats to its national security.

On the morning of September 13, 1985, Air Force Major Doug Pearson smashed through the sound barrier in his

F-15. Pointed almost directly upward more than seven miles above the Pacific Ocean, he tapped a little red button on the side of his control stick, and released a missile strapped to the belly of his plane. The missile blazed out of sight, leaving the earth's atmosphere quickly and reaching a speed of 13,000 miles per second. Pearson wondered if it would hit anything.

The mission was classified, so Pearson had developed a code with the folks back at Edwards Air Force Base: The radioman would tell him to level off at a certain altitude if his missile struck its target, an obsolete scientific probe orbiting 345 miles over Hawaii. As it happened, the code wasn't necessary. When Pearson checked in a few minutes after firing, he could hear cheering in the background from the control room.

It was the one time an American pilot had ever destroyed an object in outer space. People still talk about Pearson as the country's first "space ace." He remains its only space ace. A few weeks after the satellite was destroyed, Congress banned further tests. "We had hoped to conduct more," recalls Pearson, now a general. "But politics were what they were, and the nation decided to go another way."

A Monroe Doctrine for the Heavens

Space is the next great frontier of military innovation, but for 17 years the nation has gone another way. It has squandered a remarkable opportunity that may not be available much longer. Rather than move rapidly to build on the success of Pearson and many others involved in the military use of space, the United States has refused to develop technologies that will be essential to national security in the 21st century, from anti-satellite (ASAT) missiles like Pearson's to space-based lasers that can destroy ICBMs [intercontinental ballistic missiles] right after they've left their launch pads.

Democrats ridiculed Ronald Reagan's Strategic Defense Initiative as "Star Wars," and not much has changed: Rep. Dennis Kucinich, Democrat of Ohio, introduced the Space Preservation Act of 2002, which would ban weapons from space "for the benefit of all humankind." The language of his bill is so broad that it would effectively reinstate the now-defunct Anti-Ballistic Missile Treaty. It would also block construction of the limited missile-defense system now underway at Fort Greely in Alaska, as well as a sea-based system whose development the Pentagon says it may now accelerate.

That's because ABMs that intercept their targets above the atmosphere—all of them, basically—may reasonably be deemed weapons in space. (ICBMs are weapons in space, too, but they don't engage anything until their warheads dive back into the earth.) With the ABM Treaty at last finding its deserved place on the ash heap of history, however, we now have an unprecedented occasion to rethink U.S. military strategy in space. What the country needs is an aggressive commitment to achieving space control—a kind of Monroe Doctrine for the heavens, opening them to the peaceful purposes of commerce and science but closing them to anything that threatens American national security. The United States today is the undisputed leader in space technology, but the gap between our capabilities and those of potential adversaries won't remain so wide forever. The time for bold action is now.

Force Enhancement

The military space age arguably began during the Second World War, when 1,400 German V-2 rockets rained down on England. The V-2s did not do an enormous amount of physical damage, but they did terrify the public and highlight the revolutionary potential of space weapons. "The significance of this demonstration of German skill and ingenuity lies in the fact that it makes complete nonsense out of strategic frontiers, mountains, and river barriers," said CBS newsman Edward R. Murrow from London.

> *What the country needs is an aggressive commitment to achieving space control.*

The Pentagon began to exploit the vast emptiness of space soon after. Military satellites have been in orbit for more than 40 years. In this sense, the militarization of space is old hat. Today, in fact, the armed services rely on space so much that they simply couldn't function as they currently do without access to it. Satellites facilitate communications, monitor enemy activity, and detect missile launches. Their surveillance capabilities are astounding: The KH-11 supposedly can spot objects six inches in size from hundreds of miles up. These functions were critical to the success of American campaigns against Iraq and Serbia in the 1990s, and they are essential to operations in Afghanistan.

Even seemingly mundane uses of space have military value. The Global Positioning System is well known to civilian navigators, but it was designed for military navigational purposes, such as helping cruise missiles locate their targets and special-ops units find their rally points. On June 6, 1944, General Eisenhower surely would have appreciated a weather forecast of the type we now routinely get from satellites via local TV and radio broadcasts. On September 11, 2001, it was the space-enabled transmission of cell-phone signals and instant news that helped Todd Beamer and the other passengers of United Flight 93 prevent an already catastrophic day from turning even worse.

> *For arms-control fanatics . . . space is a kind of sanctuary.*

These are all examples of "force enhancement," to use Pentagon parlance. By generating and channeling information, space-based assets help earthbound soldiers, sailors, and pilots improve their performance. Yet the United States will also need tools of "force application"—weapons that act against adversaries directly in and from space, for both offensive and defensive purposes. What our country requires, in short, is the weaponization of outer space.

Trimmed Budgets

This already would have occurred in at least limited form, but for the mulish opposition of arms-control liberals. Reagan's SDI routinely struggled for funding in the 1980s and early 1990s, and then went on life support during the Clinton administration. The budget for ground-based ABMs was slashed by nearly 80 percent in Clinton's first year—defense contractors even had their system-development bids returned to them unopened. The Brilliant Pebbles program, an outgrowth of SDI that would have placed a swarm of maneuverable interceptors in orbit, was eliminated completely. "These actions effectively destroyed the nation's spaced-based missile-defense options for the following decade," says Henry Cooper, who ran the Strategic Defense Initiative Organization at the Pentagon during the first Bush administration.

The budgets of other programs, such as the ASAT technology tested by Pearson in 1985, were essentially trimmed to death. In 1990, Democrats in Congress forbade ASAT laser testing (the Republican majority let the ban lapse in 1995). The Army worked on ground-based ASAT missiles through the 1990s, and by 1997 its tests were starting to show real promise. The next year, however, Clinton had a test of his own to run—the line-item veto, since ruled unconstitutional by the Supreme Court—and he used it against the Army program. "We could have had something online," says Steven Lambakis of the National Institute for Public Policy. "Now we'd be forced to cobble together an emergency response if we really needed to knock out a satellite."

The United States soon will have at least a residual ASAT capability—any national missile-defense system that can shoot down ICBMs also can obliterate satellites. What we don't have, however, is a growing architecture of space-based weapons along the lines of what Reagan began to describe in his visionary SDI speech in 1983. [In] May [2002], Senate Democrats passed big cuts to ground-based missile defense, which is humdrum compared with space-based lasers and the like—and the White House has not yet beaten back even this challenge.

What Space Is

The wrangling over weapons and budgets stems from a fundamental confusion over what space is and how we should use it. From the standpoint of physics, space begins about 60 miles above sea level, which is roughly the minimum height a satellite must attain to achieve orbit. In this sense, space is just another medium, much like land, water, and air, with its own special rules of operation. For military purposes, however, space is more: It's the ultimate high ground, a flank from above whose importance, for those able to gain access to it, may represent the critical difference in future conflicts.

For arms-control fanatics, however, space is a kind of sanctuary, and putting weapons in it poses an unconscionable threat. U.N. secretary general Kofi Annan has called for ensuring "that outer space remains weapons-free." Theresa Hitchens of the Center for Defense Information warns of threats to "global stability" and "the potential for starting a damaging and destabilizing space race." With space, there's always the sense that weapons violate some pristine nature. This is clearly one of the sentiments behind the Kucinich bill. Yet it is exactly wrong—there should be weapons way up there because then there will be fewer of them right down here.

> *The private sector also requires a secure space environment.*

Space power is now in its infancy, just as air power was when the First World War erupted in 1914. Back then, military planes initially were used to observe enemy positions. There was an informal camaraderie among pilots; Germans and French would even wave when they flew by each other. Yet it wasn't long before the reality of war took hold and they began shooting. The skies were not to be a safe haven.

The lesson for space is that some country inevitably will move to seize control of it, no matter how much money the United States sinks into feel-good projects like the International Space Station. Americans have been caught napping before, as when the Soviet Union shocked the world with Sputnik in 1957. In truth, the United States could have beaten the Soviets to space but for a deliberate slow-down strategy that was meant to foster sunny relations with the world's other superpower.

The Importance of Controlling Space

The United States is the world's frontrunner in space, with about 110 military satellites in operation, compared with about 40 for Russia and 20 for the rest of the world. Yet a leadership role in space is not the same as dominance, and the United States today lacks the ability to defend its assets against rudimentary ASAT technology or to deny other countries their own weapons in space. No country appears to be particularly close to putting weapons in orbit, though the Chinese are expected to launch their first astronaut in the next year or two and they're working hard to upgrade their military space capabilities. "It would be a mistake to underestimate the rapidity with which other states are beginning to use space-based systems to enhance their security," says the just-released annual report of the Stockholm International Peace Research Institute. At a U.N. disarmament conference two years ago, Chinese officials called for a treaty to keep weapons out of space—a possible sign that what they really want is some time to play catch-up.

The private sector also requires a secure space environment. When the Galaxy IV satellite failed in 1998, paging services shut down, affecting an estimated 44 million customers. Banks and credit-card companies also were affected, along with a few television and radio stations. . . . A nuclear explosion in low orbit could disable scores of satellites and wreak havoc on modern economies everywhere—an example of space-age terrorism.

Plenty of people inside the government already recognize how much the United States relies on space. There's a U.S. Space Command headquartered in Colorado Springs, and each branch of the military is to some extent involved in space power. In 1999, secretary of defense William Cohen called space power "as important to the nation as land, sea, and air power." His successor, Donald Rumsfeld, chaired a commission on space and national security right before joining the Bush administration. The panel's report, issued last year [in 2001], warned of a "Space Pearl Harbor" if the country doesn't develop "new military capabilities."

> **//** *The goal would be to make the heavens safe for capitalism and science while also protecting the national security of the United States.* **//**

While Cohen's rhetoric was fine, his boss, Bill Clinton, didn't seem to agree with it. Rumsfeld is friendly to the notion of space power, but President Bush so far hasn't talked much about it. When Bush gave his missile-defense speech at the National Defense University [in 2001], he spoke of land-, sea-, and air-based defenses—but made no mention of space. "A lot of us noticed that," says one Air Force officer.

The Rumsfeld commission also emphasized defense: how to protect American satellites from foreign enemies. It had almost nothing to say about offense: how to use space for projecting American power around the globe. The commission was a creature of consensus, so this does not necessarily represent Rumsfeld's own thinking. And defense certainly is important. Military satellites are tempting targets because they're so crucial to the United States in so many ways. They are protected by their remoteness, but not much else. Their frail bodies and predictable flight paths are a skeet shoot compared with hitting speedy ICBMs, an ability that the United States is just starting to master. They're also vulnerable to jamming and hacking. Hardening their exteriors, providing them with some maneuverability, and having launch-on-demand replacements available are all key ingredients to national security. Yet defense doesn't win wars. In the future, the mere act of protecting these assets won't be enough to preserve American military superiority in space.

Intellectual and Political Pressure Is Needed

In addition to an assortment of high-tech hardware, the United States could use an Alfred Thayer Mahan for the 21st century. In 1890, Mahan was a captain in the Navy when the first edition of his book, *The Influence of Sea Power on World History*, was published. Today it ranks among the classic texts of military theory. Mahan argued that nations achieve greatness only if they dominate the seas and their various geographic "pressure points," holding up the example of the British Royal Navy. One of Mahan's early readers was a young man named Theodore Roosevelt, who began to apply these ideas while working in the Department of the Navy during the 1890s, and later as president. Mahanian principles shook the country loose from its traditional strategy of coastal defense and underwrote a period of national dynamism, which included the annexation of Hawaii, victory in the Spanish-American War, and the construction of the Panama Canal.

No writer has clearly become the Mahan of space, though one candidate is Everett C. Dolman, a professor at the Air Force's School of Advanced Airpower Studies, in Alabama. Dolman's new book *Astropolitik* offers a grand strategy that would have the United States "endeavor at once to seize military control of low-Earth orbit" and impose "a police blockade of all current spaceports, monitoring and controlling all traffic both in and out." Dolman identifies low-Earth orbit as a chokepoint in the sense of Mahan—anybody who wants access to space must pass through it. "The United States should grab this vital territory now, when there's no real competition for it," Dolman tells me. "Once we're there, we can make sure the entry cost for anybody else wanting to achieve space control is too high.

Whoever takes space will dominate Earth."

Dolman would benefit from a political benefactor. Mahan enjoyed the patronage of Roosevelt, who took a scholar's ideas and turned them into policies. Space has a number of advocates within the military bureaucracy, mostly among its younger members. It does not have a political champion, with the possible exception of Sen. Bob Smith, a New Hampshire Republican who has made the subject a personal passion. Smith calls space America's "next Manifest Destiny" and believes the Department of Defense should establish an independent Space Force to serve alongside the Army, Navy, and Air Force. Smith, however, may not stay in the Senate much longer, facing stiff political challenges at home.

With the right mix of intellectual firepower and political muscle, the United States could achieve what Dolman calls "hegemonic control" of space. The goal would be to make the heavens safe for capitalism and science while also protecting the national security of the United States. "Only those spacecraft that provide advance notice of their mission and flight plan would be permitted in space," writes Dolman. Anything else would be shot down.

That may sound like 21st-century imperialism, which, in essence, it would be. But is that so bad? Imagine that the United States currently maintained a battery of space-based lasers. India and Pakistan could inch toward nuclear war over Kashmir, only to be told that any attempt by either side to launch a missile would result in a boost-phase blast from outer space. Without taking sides, the United States would immediately defuse a tense situation and keep the skies above Bombay and Karachi free of mushroom clouds. Moreover, Israel would receive protection from Iran and Iraq, Taiwan from China, and Japan and South Korea from the mad dictator north of the DMZ [demilitarized zone]. The United States would be covered as well, able not merely to deter aggression, but also to defend against it.

National security always has been an expensive proposition, and there is no getting around the enormous costs posed by a robust system of space-based weaponry. It would take a supreme act of national will to make it a reality. We've done it before: Winning the Cold War required laying out trillions of dollars, much of it on machines, missiles, and warheads that never saw live combat. Seizing control of space also would cost trillions, but it would lead to a world made immeasurably safer for America and what it values.

7

The United States Should Not Militarize Space

Loring Wirbel

Loring Wirbel is editorial director for communications at CMP Media, a media company based in New York and London. He is on the board of directors of the Global Network Against Weapons and Nuclear Power in Space.

The United States increasingly relies on space-based intelligence and communications systems in waging war. The nation is also developing weapons systems that go beyond missile defense and ensure its ability to strike first in a nuclear war. America's unilateral control of space is maintained by a subtly pressured global consensus. This worldwide deference to America is based on a misguided belief by other nations that U.S. imperial control is the best option for providing geopolitical stability and protection from rogue states and terrorism. Activists must oppose this unilateral domination of space.

The military space agencies have made no secret of their desire for both domination of the planet, and "negation" of other nations' space capabilities. But they would rather the public not fully grasp that each time a precision Joint Direct Attack Munition, or JDAM, guided by the Global Positioning System, was dropped on an Iraqi city, the U.S. was waging a war from space. Each time an Unmanned Aerial Vehicle fed intelligence to the Global Broadcast System satellite network, the U.S. was waging a war from space. Each time signals intelligence satellites updated the coordinates of Ba'ath party leaders, the U.S. was waging a war from space.

Forgive the legions of embedded reporters traveling alongside invading U.S. forces in Iraq for assuming the March [2003] assault was an earthbound affair. Military leaders convening in Colorado Springs in early April agreed that the attack on Iraq utilized space to an extent never before seen in modern warfare. But to the media, blinded by dust storms while fawning over Marine and Army divisions on the march from Kuwait to Baghdad, the role of space was hard to determine. And that is precisely how the directors of Air Force Space Command and the National Reconnaissance Office would like it.

> *// The notion of preemptive assault from space has found . . . favor in the aftermath of the attack on Iraq. //*

As military space doctrine has evolved and sharpened from Kosovo to Colombia, from Afghanistan to Iraq, a growing number of peace activists have grasped that the mission of preventing the weaponization of space involves far more than opposing the missile-defense weapons of the Missile Defense Agency. Space dominance entails not just the weapons physically placed in space, but weapon systems enabled through elaborate networks of intelligence, targeting, and communication systems, which constitute a web of dominance in orbit around the Earth. When these networks are wedded to a doctrine of total preventive war, spelled out in the September 2002 "National Security Strategy of the United States," they constitute a blueprint for permanent war to assure U.S. global superiority.

Nuclear Weapons in Space

In the aftermath of the war on Iraq the Air Force Space Command tightened collaboration with its partner, Strategic Command, to bring the nuclear weapons infrastructure into the new space-dominance paradigm. The two organizations were slated to meet at Offut Air Force Base in August 2003, to ponder the implications of a new Defense Department program called "Operationally Responsive Spacelift," or ORS. The ORS plan calls for abandoning joint work with NASA on a lightweight Orbital Space Plane, in favor of a heavy-lift military space plane which could serve as a manned assault or reconnaissance vehicle. ORS entails using retired Minuteman-III rockets for a variety of new missions, including first-strike assault in which the missiles could be outfitted with either nuclear or conventional weapons. Air Force Space Command is talking about the development of a new Minuteman-IV missile, which would borrow mobile basing strategies from the plans for the original MX missile, while using the earth-penetrating nuclear weapons now being discussed for possible development at Los Alamos National Labs.

In fact, the notion of preemptive assault from space has found such favor in the aftermath of the attack on Iraq, the Air Force's Office of Space Operations and Integration (which proudly sports the new logo of "Air and Space Operations—The Superiority Complex"), is talking openly of using first-strike attacks on airfields and missile fields as a more effective substitute for strategic missile defense. In the early days of the Bush administration, activists had to struggle to make the case that ballistic missile defense was a first-strike technology, not a means of defense against non-existent threats. By the end of the war on Iraq, the military openly admitted to looking for the most effective first-strike weapons it could find, whether those weapons were missile-defense rockets and lasers, or strike aircraft used for aerial assault.

Normalizing the Use of Space

By normalizing the use of space and rendering it invisible, the Bush administration could maintain the pretense that its interest in Star Wars weapons and space supremacy appears to have shifted to the back burner. The second half of 2002 appeared to be a slack time for space. The Space-Based Laser Office within the Missile Defense Agency was closed, and the federal-level Space Command went through a Pentagon merger, leaving only specific Space Commands for Air Force, Army, and Navy to head up service-specific space missions. The melding of the U.S. Space Command into the Strategic Command on October 1, 2002, would seem to underscore the message that Donald Rumsfeld's promise in early 2001 of making dominance of planetary space a key military goal has fallen victim to terrestrial practicalities.

Nothing could be further from the truth. The constant use of space during the pre-invasion buildup in Iraq, and the three-week ground assault that followed, shows that the model of space warfare has been perfected, using a combination of permanent and "virtual" space-support bases in Oman, Qatar, Bahrain, Eritrea, Diego Garcia, and other nations. But the notion that space constitutes a special dimension has fallen into disfavor. Since the U.S. already considers itself sole proprietor of global sea and air lanes, it is only natural that it manages all orbital and sub-orbital space on the planet, and there is not nearly so much of a reason to boast about the concept, as there was ten years ago when the dominance theory was in its infancy.

Learning by Doing

In contrast to the heyday of the 1990s, when the U.S. Space Command released documents like *Vision for 2020* and *Long Range Plan* which boasted of "space-based force multipliers" in all theatres of battle, the U.S. military has spent the last two years in a quieter mode, learning by doing. Real-time support of battle groups by space platforms has been perfected by deploying tactical space units as part of a "Forward Operating Location" strategy of pre-positioning experts in intelligence and communications to global hot spots.

> ❝ *The Commission [to Assess U.S. National Security Space Management] warned of a 'Pearl Harbor in space' unless total U.S. domination of the planet through unilateral control of space was achieved.* ❞

Secretary of Defense Donald Rumsfeld let the Commission to Assess United States National Security Space Management and Organization do the talking on space supremacy on his behalf in the very early days of the Bush administration. The Commission warned of a "Pearl Harbor in space" unless total U.S. domination of the planet through unilateral control of space was achieved. This view was reinforced in late September 2002, when the White House released its more general national security policy document that justified U.S. efforts to establish a global empire and wage continuous preemptive war to preserve dominance.

> *Space-based military networks and missile-defense weapons become merely two more arrows in the quiver of global hegemony.*

The Bush team also relied on Peter Teets, Director of the National Reconnaissance Office (NRO) and former COO [chief operating officer] of Lockheed Martin, to do some public boasting in numerous public speeches about how successful the war in Afghanistan had been in proving the viability of space as a force multiplier. Teets, who serves a unique new role as chief Pentagon procurement officer for space, in charge of a $68 billion space budget, said that Afghanistan reinforced the message previously given by Teets' predecessor Keith Hall regarding space dominance: "We have it, we like it, and we're going to keep it."

NASA Administrator Sean O'Keefe has proudly touted his own agency's involvement in the Afghanistan war, describing at the 2002 National Space Symposium the use of the Sea-WiFS satellite for tracking Taliban troops. O'Keefe has not bothered with the niceties of preserving artificial distinctions between Pentagon and NASA space use, particularly given his own history as Navy secretary and comptroller in the Pentagon. In return, the Defense Department has made NASA an integral part of national security space networks. In early September 2002, Teets announced the creation of the Transformational Communications Office, a joint office of NRO, NASA, and various military and intelligence agencies, aiming for a unified secure communications network.

"Permanent Pre-Eminence"

Yet given this central role for space-based forces, why was U.S. Space Command apparently given the heave-ho? Even conservative think tanks which favor a high-tech "revolution in military affairs," but question nuclear weapons, had trouble with the Space Command/Strategic Command merger. The STRATFOR study group released an analysis last July [2002] suggesting that Rumsfeld was tying Space Command to a nuclear dinosaur.

Such analyses assume that Bush has lost interest in nuclear weapons since cutting some informal arms-reduction deals with [Russian president] Vladimir Putin. But the conclusions of the Nuclear Posture Review, as well as Rumsfeld's suggestion that the Missile Defense Agency explore nuclear warheads for missile interceptor rockets, should convince skeptics that the Bush administration sees nuclear weapons as both central to space dominance, and useable in strategies to attain global supremacy.

In this scenario, combining Strategic Command and Space Command make perfect sense. The global gladiator is going to use all available tools to achieve what arms analyst Michael Klare calls "permanent pre-eminence." Space-based military networks and missile-defense weapons become merely two more arrows in the quiver of global hegemony. Anyone who misconceives Star Wars weapons as defensively "protecting" the U.S. homeland from rogue missiles, has not been paying attention to the evolution of modern military doctrine.

The final, frightening aspect in this combat-command shell game is the establishment of a new domestic command, the Northern Command, which will take over facilities of the Space Command at Peterson Air Force Base in Colorado Springs. Gen. Ed Eberhart, former head of the Space Command, has moved to Northern Command, and already has begun to talk about removing elements of the Posse Comitatus Act that prevent the military from serving in domestic law enforcement roles. Because Northern Command will have access to the base of high-tech tools developed by aerospace corporations for the Space Command, it will represent the cutting edge of surveillance, analysis, and data-mining tools that will exploit the holes in privacy laws left by passage of the USA Patriot Act. We shall explore later how the corporate community is taking advantage of this shift.

Space Intelligence

Technical intelligence, once the realm of the National Security Agency and specialized CIA divisions, has since the Reagan era become a joint venture of the NSA, the nation's electronic-listening agency, and the forementioned NRO, manager of the nation's spy satellites. Either of these agencies on their own dwarf the size of the CIA. Together, they control a visible annual budget well in excess of $10 billion. Since the mid-1990s, the NRO and NSA have shared resources through the establishment of joint bases called Regional SIGINT Operations Centers, or RSOCs.

Although these agencies' budgets are classified, what is known about their annual expenditures tells only half the story. The biggest shift in NSA and NRO doctrine since the end of the Cold War is that both agencies have kept the bulk of their resources intact, but have shined their focus to providing real-time intelligence to U.S. forces involved in direct tactical battles, a strategy called "serving the warfighter." Much of the effort at getting intelligence from primary spy satellites and ground networks to tactical battle groups has come, not from NSA or NRO budgets, but from tactical intelligence budget programs called TENCAP (Tactical Exploitation of National Capabilities) and TIARA (Tactical Intelligence and Related Activities). When the billions of dollars in tactical intelligence programs are added to NSA and NRO agency budgets, it is reasonable to assume that exploitation of space for power projection consumes half or more of the nation's estimated $38 billion annual intelligence budget.

> *The U.S. no longer disguises the fact that it considers itself the planetary boss.*

NRO manages imaging satellites in space that capture data in both visible-lightrange (Keyhole/Kennan) and radar wavelengths, using synthetic aperture radar (Lacrosse). Together, these satellite systems are used to build a "multispectral" database for use by the National Imagery and Mapping Agency, which can then be applied to air-breathing vehicles ranging from cruise missiles to unpiloted aerial reconnaissance vehicles, or UAVs. The imaging satellites will be augmented in 2005 by a new family of geosynchronous satellites built by Boeing, dubbed "8X," or Future Imagery Architecture. These highly classified satellites represent the most expensive military procurement program in history, with each satellite priced at several billion dollars, excluding cost of the launch vehicle.

NRO also is lobbying heavily to get Congress to approve a multi-agency Space-Based Radar. This would represent a vast improvement over Lacrosse, because it would allow active tracking of moving targets from space, what Teets called a "JSTARS weapons program in space" (JSTARS is a radar-surveillance plane used in standoff "deep-strike" attack).

NRO's signals-intelligence, or electronic-listening satellites, went through a significant revolution in the 1990s, moving to new families of geosynchronous satellites dubbed Mercury, Mentor, and Trumpet. These satellites used unfurlable antennas built by TRW and subcontractors, which could expand in space to cover the length of three football fields. The performance of such satellites proved so impressive, the NSA accelerated programs to close down several ground-based antenna fields, while moving others to remote unmanned status.

> *In short, it becomes difficult to discern tactical missile defense from overall strategies of offense used in preemptive war.*

Again, these satellites will be upgraded around 2004 or 2005 by a new monster called Intruder, an element in the Integrated Overhead SIGINT Architecture (IOSA) program. Boeing once again serves as prime contractor for this satellite. It is interesting to note that NRO was pondering a move to a new architecture of many smaller satellites operating in tandem, in a program called IOSA-2. In two separate lobbying campaigns in the mid-1990s and early 21st century, Congress killed NRO's interest in small satellites after intense lobbying by Boeing and Lockheed Martin, which argued that support of gargantuan geosynchronous spy satellites was necessary for national security, a prime example of classified pork barrel politics.

Total Situational Awareness

Does the collaboration of NSA and NRO in this field constitute a gross violation of civil liberties, as critics of the Echelon program charge? In theory, yes, since satellites can scoop up transmissions in virtually any frequency band. In reality, the agencies do not have nearly the storage space or human analysts to go over even a tiny percentage of their "take." What is more alarming, however, is the degree to which the products of the new collaboration have been fed directly to tactical battle groups, raising the possibility that any future skirmish that U.S.

forces are involved in, becomes a "turkey shoot" by definition.

In a series of experiments begun at Schriever Air Force Base in the mid-1990s, the Space Command practiced transmitting "fused" intelligence information from NSA and NRO to battleships, fighter jet cockpits, and individual Special Operations soldiers in the field, under a classified series of programs dubbed the Talon missions, Talon Shield, Talon Knight, etc. The program went "live" in July 1996. It was expanded to cover UAVs during the Kosovo bombing, using island bases off the Dalmatian coast, along with specialized air fields in Hungary and Albania.

The Pentagon used the Plan Colombia Forward Operating Location (FOL) strategy in 2000 as a model for later battles. Special bases were set up in El Salvador, Ecuador, Antigua, and Curacao, which served the roles of space downlinks, signals intelligence antenna fields, and UAV airfields. These were used to create a "total situational awareness" environment for Colombia, where space directly served soldiers on the ground.

> *Developing a strategy of opposition requires, at its base, absolute non-compliance with the politics of unilateral domination of the planet.*

In Afghanistan, FOLs were renamed "Forward Operating Bases," reflecting the semi-permanent nature of bases both in-country, and in neighboring nations such as Uzbekistan and Tajikistan. Capabilities were expanded by adding the broadband information-distribution capabilities of a network called Global Broadcast Service. GBS, in partial operation since 1996, uses the Navy's UHF Follow-On satellite to transmit a mix of voice, data, and video streams to any location with a small satellite dish. Some content is as benign as the Pentagon's version of a CNN broadcast, while other content is as sensitive as the NSA's Binocular intelligence distribution database. When American troops in Afghanistan utilized the GBS system on board the UFO satellites, Teets told the 2002 Space Symposium, Special Operations forces operating on horseback in southern Afghanistan could receive instant video feeds from Predator UAV flights in other parts of the country.

This example shows the important role played by commu-

nications and navigation satellites in enabling first-strike warfare. These systems, often considered benign by those studying
military space, can be exploited to allow far more effective preemptive strikes.

GPS as a Weapon of War

The case of the Global Positioning System is particularly in-
structive. For 20 years, activists have fought a losing battle to
convince the public that GPS is first and foremost a weapon of
war. Since GPS receivers are available for virtually any car or hik-
ing kit, its transition to a civilian technology seems complete.
But with every step to "open" GPS frequencies to broader public use comes simultaneous efforts to add additional military-
only frequencies, or to use GPS in ways that emphasize targeting before location-finding. The widespread use of JDAM bombs
in the assault on Iraq shows that GPS now has more tactical targeting duties than position-location or strategic nuclear targeting. Gen. Lance Lord, Commander of the Air Force Space Command, quipped at the 2003 National Space Symposium that
"GPS puts the DAM [sic] in JDAM."

The Pentagon has its own evolutionary program for im-
proving GPS as a weapon of war, from the current GETS (GPS
for Enhanced Theatre Support) to the future "GPS III—Navwar"
program. All steps in the evolution assume an exclusive por-
tion of the GPS program reserved for military use, which is why
the U.S. is so anxious to prevent the European Space Agency
from going ahead with its own Galileo navigation satellite program. If space supremacy is to become a reality, neither allies
nor foes can be allowed to have the tools in common use by
the U.S. military.

Improving First-Strike Capability

Infrared satellites for missile detection have followed a similar
path. The aging Defense Support Program, or DSP, satellites
were used in passive fashion to warn of possible Soviet or Chinese missile launches. These satellites were upgraded in the
1990s under Project Alert, which could instantaneously shuttle
information about expected missile plumes to battle groups
working in other regions of the world. DSP's obvious limitations were what sparked interest in a two-tiered follow-on system, the Space-Based Infrared System, which was sold as an es-

sential element of Star Wars under the separate programs of SBIRS-High and SBIRS-Low. The fact that the SBIRS satellites can be used as elements of a first-strike system spotlights the fundamental yet unspoken problem with missile-defense: Most aspects of a national or tactical system, particularly those associated with Theatre Missile Defense, can be construed by adversaries as tools that allow more effective first strikes, rather than tools that defend against incoming missiles.

Even the various satellite systems providing communications at UHF, EHF, and SHF frequencies—DSCS, Milstar, FleetSatCom, etc.—can become tools by which to assure total dominance in any battlefield. Jam resistance and stealth characteristics added to recent communication satellite systems help to insure that the military achieves what the Long-Range Plan dubs "full-spectrum dominance."

In April 2003, the NRO's Teets described a new $9 billion program to further enhance satellite systems, while unifying the networks of NRO, NASA, and the Defense Information Systems Agency. NRO plans on a new family of broadband, packet-switched satellites to give space military networks the power of a classified Internet. This system, the Transformational-Satellite or T-SAT system, will be augmented by a new class of high-latitude NRO satellites called the Advanced Polar System. Teets said that the two new systems, T-SAT and APS, are designed to communicate directly with new military satellites already under development at DISA—the Advanced Extremely-High-Frequency satellite (a successor to Milstar), the Wideband Gapfiller satellite, and the Multi-User Objective System, or MUOS satellite.

Military-Corporate Cooperation

The U.S. Space Command may have come to an end last October [2002], but the mission statements described in its documents remain as active as ever. In fact, operations on the ground still remain similar to those present prior to the agency's merger into Strategic Command at Offut Air Force Base. The service-specific commands— Army Space Command, Navy Space Command, Air Force Space Command—remain headquartered at Peterson AFB in Colorado Springs, operating out of the same offices they used when a unified space command was in charge of all three. Occupying the U.S. Space Command office space at Peterson is the new Northern Command, boasting the same top management formerly assigned to U.S. Space Command.

This gives those military contractors with an inside track on space contracts continued right of first refusal for surveillance and data-mining systems designed for Northern Command and its civilian equivalent, the Department of Homeland Security. Raytheon Corp., Oracle Corp., and other large companies with long histories of working with NSA and NRO are tightly involved in programs for biometric scanning at U.S. borders, luggage scanning for the Transportation Security Agency and similar U.S.-based monitoring programs.

Often, companies show a high degree of innovation in how they combine operations. Raytheon, for example, established a large, highly secure facility across the street from the Buckley AFB intelligence base in Aurora, where it began processing outsourced intelligence information for the NSA and NRO in 1998. In 2000, Raytheon set up a secure Web-hosting operation for corporations in the same location. And in 2002, Raytheon created a division to build ground stations for a joint NRO/NIMA/NASA weather satellite called N-POESS—again, located in the same unified Aurora facility where it performs NRO and NSA spy work while hosting corporate Web sites.

It is ironic that so much attention has been paid to the Defense Advanced Research Projects Agency's Information Awareness Office, under the management of former National Security Adviser John Poindexter. The office has talked of fusing databases representing several sources of intelligence information, but has been forced to pledge several generations of tests on non-specific data, in order to prove to Congress it is not violating civil liberties. Meanwhile, however, defense contractors have moved data-mining tools directly from Space Command duties that supported the assault on Iraq, to Northern Command and Department of Homeland Security duties supporting domestic intelligence agencies. Northrop Grumman, for example, has moved a tool called Web-TAS, developed in conjunction with the Air Force Research Labs, out of early trials at the Combined Air Operations Center at Prince Sultan Air Base in Saudi Arabia, and out to local and regional police intelligence agencies within the U.S. and worldwide.

Using Space to Achieve Dominance

The common thread of government doctrine, updating and expanding what once was a Space Command–specific doctrine, can be found in Bush's June 1, 2002, speech at West Point, and in the September 20, 2002, document on national security policy. The U.S. no longer disguises the fact that it considers itself the planetary boss. Programs for militarily utilizing a particular medium—space, air, sea—are based on the assumption that the U.S. is the only nation with the unilateral right to control such venues, and that if other nations attempt to share control of space or sea lanes they must be halted by force.

> // *Advocates for peace in space must oppose not only weapons in space, but those military systems in space that serve unilateral dominance.* //

This dominance operates through a planetary consensus system of global deference to the United States, rather than through the naked exercise of power present in the British empire of a century ago. Martin Walker, senior fellow at the World Policy Institute, calls this a "virtual empire," because American power "is so evident and sweeping that it does not need to be formally exercised . . . [direct] rule is hardly necessary when so many of the goods that flow from the virtual empire are too desirable or essential to be adjured." When nations directly confront this unwritten rule, as France, Germany, and Russia attempted to do within the UN Security Council in mid-March [2003], they are simply ignored, and later condemned for failure to acknowledge the legitimacy of hegemony.

This "planetary consensus" bears some resemblance to the "Washington Consensus" on economic policy of the mid-1990s, because both operate tacitly and subtly, yet assume that any fundamental challenge to the consensus serves as evidence that those challenging it must be mentally disturbed. Such a consensus was demanded of allies and partners in issues of space militarization and weaponization long before the assault on Iraq. Initial European opposition to re-entry-phase missile-defense weapons in 2001 all but disappeared in the aftermath of the September 11 attacks. China, which had pledged to lead an anti-space-dominance coalition in the UN, quickly forgot its promises after being admitted into the World Trade Organization. France and Russia now face tremendous pressure in the aftermath of the UN Security Council breach to "get with the program" and recognize the new unilateralism. If American allies do not speak out about ground-based missile-defense weapons now, why should they speak out about space-based weapons and the abrogation of the 1967 Outer Space Treaty five years from now?

It should be obvious to those allies by now that the Missile Defense Agency is not in place to protect the United States and allies from intermediate missiles fired by "rogue states." Missile defense instead is a means of reinforcing the military dominance created by the new precision weapons and intelligence tools utilized from space, air, and sea. While the Defense Science Board has tried to narrow the original Bush Missile Defense Agency approach of approving any form of missile-defense weapon in any venue, the choices it suggested in September 2002 are interesting for what they say about missile-defense goals. DSB suggested the top two priorities for MDA should be ground-based interceptors and sea-based theatre missile defense. The kinetic-kill ground-based interceptors are precisely those systems that warrant near-term deployment of X-band radars, control networks run out of Fort Greely, Alaska, the SBIRS infrared sensor system, and other elements that have a dual role in aiding U.S. tactical intelligence of regional battlefields. Sea-based Theatre Missile Defense, meanwhile, is based on the Aegis missile cruiser, its SPY-1 radar, and a family of short-range missiles which would prove very useful in challenging Chinese naval power in any battles for Taiwan. In short, it becomes difficult to discern tactical missile defense from overall strategies of offense used in preemptive war.

A Strategy of Opposition

In some senses, the demise of the Space Command hurts activists, since it deprives us of a lightning rod that helped direct attention to the overall aggressive nature of American policy in the neo-imperialist era. Space supremacy goals are just as active, but have been subsumed into a Strategic Command infrastructure whose use of space is so commonplace it becomes part of the background noise.

Peace activists also are not helped by the "planetary consensus" of leaders of nations who assume that a world under U.S. imperial control is the best one imaginable, if nations are to be protected from failed states and sub-state terrorists. That is why it is all the more crucial for activists in this country to join together with those in other nations. Accepting a planetary boss is a bad bargain for all concerned. The boss will demand physical control of all resources globally, will seek to own all economic trade routes, and will insist on absolute exemption from transnational agencies that might restrict its action. (These include not only the International Criminal Court, but, ironically, the World Trade Organization, whose rulings on foreign corporate taxes may demonstrate to the United States that the Frankenstein it helped create has turned with a vengeance on its master.)

Developing a strategy of opposition requires, at its base, absolute non-compliance with the politics of unilateral domination of the planet. Preemptive war must be opposed not only in Iraq, but everywhere. Missile-defense weapons must be opposed not only because they will not work or are too expensive, but because they constitute first-strike weapons.

But opposition to space supremacy cannot stop there. Some arms-control advocates insist we should draw the line on space weaponization, while accepting the fact that space militarization has been a fact of life for 40 years. In a recent policy paper, Philip Coyle, of the Center for Defense Information, and John Rhinelander, former vice chairman of the Arms Control Association, argue correctly that planetary space can never again become a "sanctuary," the equivalent of Antarctica. They are right: Military satellites for communications and intelligence are unlikely to ever go away.

The appropriate line to draw is on the issue of destabilization and unilateralism. Space Command, NRO, and NSA, have stated in public numerous times in the past decade that their mission no longer involves treaty verification, if it ever did. Instead, their business is to re-target strategic platforms for tactical purposes, serving the warfighter with real-time information that helps insure total tactical victory in any region. When seen in the light of the new global supremacy policy, such a mission is obviously dangerous. Advocates for peace in space must oppose not only weapons in space, but those military systems in space that serve unilateral dominance. This implies opposing more than half of the space systems fielded by the U.S. military. But to strive for anything less is to provide tacit support for the new planetary consensus supporting U.S. global supremacy.

8

Replacing the Space Shuttle Program Should Be a Priority

Gregg Easterbrook

Gregg Easterbrook is a senior editor of the New Republic *and a visiting fellow at the Brookings Institution.*

The space shuttle program was designed three decades ago and needs to be replaced. It is too expensive, too risky, and too big for most of its missions. Flights were originally estimated to cost $5 million in today's dollars but instead run upward of $500 million. This huge expense could be redirected into the design of a modern system that would be much safer, cheaper, and more practical for space exploration. Unfortunately, aerospace contractors are aggressively lobbying against the development of a new system because its lower operating cost would reduce their profits. The government needs to close the program immediately and begin plans for a modern, cheaper, and safer system.

A spacecraft is a metaphor of national inspiration: majestic, technologically advanced, produced at dear cost and entrusted with precious cargo, rising above the constraints of the earth. The spacecraft carries our secret hope that there is something better out there—a world where we may someday go and leave the sorrows of the past behind. The spacecraft rises toward the heavens exactly as, in our finest moments as a nation, our hearts have risen toward justice and principle. And when, for no clear reason, the vessel crumbles, as it did in 1986 with *Challenger* and last week [February 1, 2003] with *Columbia*, we falsely think the promise of America goes with it.

Unfortunately, the core problem that lay at the heart of the *Challenger* tragedy applies to the *Columbia* tragedy as well. That core problem is the space shuttle itself. For 20 years, the American space program has been wedded to a space-shuttle system that is too expensive, too risky, too big for most of the ways it is used, with budgets that suck up funds that could be invested in a modern system that would make space flight cheaper and safer. The space shuttle is impressive in technical terms, but in financial terms and safety terms no project has done more harm to space exploration. With hundreds of launches to date, the American and Russian manned space programs have suffered just three fatal losses in flight—and two were space-shuttle calamities. This simply must be the end of the program.

Will the Much More Expensive Effort to Build a Manned International Space Station End Too?

In cost and justification, it's as dubious as the shuttle. The two programs are each other's mirror images. The space station was conceived mainly to give the shuttle a destination, and the shuttle has been kept flying mainly to keep the space station serviced. Three crew members—Expedition Six, in NASA argot—remain aloft on the space station. Probably a Russian rocket will need to go up to bring them home.[1] The wisdom of replacing them seems dubious at best. This second shuttle loss means NASA must be completely restructured—if not abolished and replaced with a new agency with a new mission.

Why Did NASA Stick with the Space Shuttle So Long?

Though the space shuttle is viewed as futuristic, its design is three decades old. The shuttle's main engines, first tested in the late 1970s, use hundreds more moving parts than do new rocket-motor designs. The fragile heat-dissipating tiles were designed before breakthroughs in materials science. Until recently, the flight-deck computers on the space shuttle used old 8086 chips from the early 1980s, the sort of pre-Pentium electronics no self-

---

1. The Expedition Six crew was returned to earth on May 3, 2003.

respecting teenager would dream of using for a video game.

Most important, the space shuttle was designed under the highly unrealistic assumption that the fleet would fly to space once a week and that each shuttle would need to be big enough to carry 50,000 lbs. of payload. In actual use, the shuttle fleet has averaged five flights a year; this year flights were to be cut back to four. The maximum payload is almost never carried. Yet to accommodate the highly unrealistic initial goals, engineers made the shuttle huge and expensive. The Soviet space program also built a shuttle, called *Buran*, with almost exactly the same dimensions and capacities as its American counterpart. *Buran* flew to orbit once and was canceled, as it was ridiculously expensive and impractical.

Capitalism, of course, is supposed to weed out such inefficiencies. But in the American system, the shuttle's expense made the program politically attractive. Originally projected to cost $5 million per flight in today's dollars, each shuttle launch instead runs to around $500 million. Aerospace contractors love the fact that the shuttle launches cost so much.

> *" This second shuttle loss means NASA must be completely restructured. "*

In two decades of use, shuttles have experienced an array of problems—engine malfunctions, damage to the heat-shielding tiles—that have nearly produced other disasters. Seeing this, some analysts proposed that the shuttle be phased out, that cargo launches be carried aboard by far cheaper, unmanned, throwaway rockets and that NASA build a small "space plane" solely for people, to be used on those occasions when men and women are truly needed in space.

Throwaway rockets can fail too. [In January 2003] a French-built Ariane exploded on lift-off. No one cared, except the insurance companies that covered the payload, because there was no crew aboard. NASA's insistence on sending a crew on every shuttle flight means risking precious human life for mindless tasks that automated devices can easily carry out. Did Israeli astronaut Ilan Ramon really have to be there to push a couple of buttons on the Mediterranean Israeli Dust Experiment, the payload package he died to accompany to space?

Switching to unmanned rockets for payload launching and a small space plane for those rare times humans are really needed would cut costs, which is why aerospace contractors have lobbied against such reform. Boeing and Lockheed Martin split roughly half the shuttle business through an Orwellian-named consortium called the United Space Alliance. It's a source of significant profit for both companies; United Space Alliance employs 6,400 contractor personnel for shuttle launches alone. Many other aerospace contractors also benefit from the space-shuttle program.

> *Though the space shuttle is viewed as futuristic, its design is three decades old.*

Any new space system that reduced costs would be, to the contractors, killing the goose that lays the golden egg. Just a few weeks ago, NASA canceled a program called the Space Launch Initiative, whose goal was to design a much cheaper and more reliable replacement for the shuttle. Along with the cancellation, NASA announced that the shuttle fleet would remain in operation until 2020, meaning that *Columbia* was supposed to continue flying into outer space even when its airframe was more than 40 years old! True, B-52s have flown as long. But they don't endure three times the force of gravity on takeoff and 2000° on re-entry.

A rational person might have laughed out loud at the thought that although school buses are replaced every decade, a spaceship was expected to remain in service for 40 years. Yet the "primes," as NASA's big contractors are known, were overjoyed when the Space Launch Initiative was canceled because it promised them lavish shuttle payments indefinitely. Of course, the contractors also worked hard to make the shuttle safe. But keeping prices up was a higher priority than having a sensible launch system.

Will NASA Whitewash Problems as It Did After *Challenger?*

The haunting fact of *Challenger* was that engineers who knew about the booster-joint problem begged NASA not to launch that day and were ignored. Later the Rogers Commission, ordered to get to the bottom of things, essentially recommended that nothing change. No NASA manager was fired; no safety systems were added to the solid rocket boosters whose explosion destroyed *Challenger;* no escape-capsule system was added to get astronauts out in a calamity, which might have helped *Columbia.* In return for failure, the shuttle program got a big budget increase. Post-*Challenger* "reforms" were left up to the very old-boy network that had created the problem in the first place and that benefited from continuing high costs.

Concerned foremost with budget politics, Congress too did its best to whitewash. Large manned-space-flight centers that depend on the shuttle are in Texas, Ohio, Florida and Alabama. Congressional delegations from these states fought frantically against a shuttle replacement. The result was years of generous funding for constituents—and now another tragedy.

The tough questions that have gone unasked about the space shuttle have also gone unasked about the space station, which generates billions in budget allocations for California, Texas, Ohio, Florida and other states. Started in 1984 and originally slated to cost $14 billion in today's dollars, the space station has already cost at least $35 billion—not counting billions more for launch costs—and won't be finished until 2008. The bottled water alone that crews use aboard the space station costs taxpayers almost half a million dollars a day. (No, that is not a misprint.) There are no scientific experiments aboard the space station that could not be done far more cheaply on unmanned probes. The only space-station research that does require crew is "life science," or studying the human body's response to space. Space life science is useful but means astronauts are on the station mainly to take one another's pulse, a pretty marginal goal for such an astronomical price.

An outsider commission is needed to investigate the *Columbia* accident—and must report to the President, not Congress, since Congress has shown itself unable to think about anything but pork barrel when it comes to space programs.[2]

For 20 years, the cart has been before the horse in U.S. space policy. NASA has been attempting complex missions involving

2. On February 1, 2003, NASA convened the Columbia Accident Investigation Board. On August 26, 2003, the independent commission released its final report to the White House, Congress, and NASA. The report found that the shuttle is not inherently unsafe but requires short-term fixes. It also found that NASA culture undermines safety.

many astronauts without first developing an affordable and dependable means to orbit. The emphasis now must be on designing an all-new system that is lower priced and reliable. And if human space flight stops for a decade while that happens, so be it. Once there is a cheaper and safer way to get people and cargo into orbit, talk of grand goals might become reality. New, less-expensive throwaway rockets would allow NASA to launch more space probes—the one part of the program that is constantly cost-effective. An affordable means to orbit might make possible a return to the moon for establishment of a research base and make possible the long-dreamed-of day when men and women set foot on Mars. But no grand goal is possible while NASA relies on the super-costly, dangerous shuttle.

In 1986 the last words transmitted from *Challenger* were in the valiant vow: "We are go at throttle up!" This meant the crew was about to apply maximum thrust, which turned out to be a fatal act. In the coming days, we will learn what the last words from *Columbia* were. Perhaps they too will reflect the valor and optimism shown by astronauts of all nations. It is time NASA and the congressional committees that supervise the agency demonstrated a tiny percentage of the bravery shown by the men and women who fly to space—by canceling the money-driven shuttle program and replacing it with something that makes sense.

9

A Plan Is Needed to Protect Earth from Asteroids and Comets

Simon P. Worden

Brigadier General Simon P. Worden is deputy director for Operations, U.S. Space Command.

The time has come to consider a more structured and organized plan for protecting the planet from near-earth objects (NEOs), including meteors, asteroids, and the tails of comets. While the threat of a large, extinction-level impact is extremely unlikely, smaller objects can impact the earth with much more frequency and cause significant damage. The potential also exists that these smaller impacts, whether at the surface or in the atmosphere, could be mistaken as a nuclear attack and trigger a nuclear war. While some cataloging of NEOs has already begun, eventually all potentially threatening objects need to de identified. Space-surveillance systems will be necessary because the existing ground-based systems are only effective in identifying large objects. To prepare for the mitigation of future NEO impacts, low-cost microsatellite missions could be used to test methods of diverting objects. To minimize international disruption, a shared early warning system needs to be completed with the purpose of warning appropriate nations of an imminent threat.

I nterest in the threat caused by natural objects ("Near-Earth Objects" or NEOs) impacting the earth or its atmosphere is growing. High-level commissions have met to consider the

Simon P. Worden, statement before the House Space and Aeronautics Subcommittee, House Science Committee, Washington, DC, October 3, 2002.

problem in such places as the United Kingdom. In the United States, NASA has devoted a few million dollars per year to studying the phenomenon. But no concrete plan exists to address the overall NEO problem.

The U.S. Department of Defense (DoD) has not perceived the NEO issue as pressing. However, DoD is assisting NASA in studying the problem. It has been DoD-developed technology, particularly in the space surveillance area, which has obtained the bulk of data we currently have on NEOs.

I have been asked to address my perspectives on the NEO threat and what should be done about it. I make the following comments not as a representative of the U.S. DoD, but rather as a scientist who has studied NEOs, and as a space expert familiar with the technologies that might be applicable to the problem.

The Threat

Two and a half months ago [in July 2002] Pakistan and India were at full alert and poised for a large-scale war, which both sides appeared ready to escalate into nuclear war. The situation has defused—for now. Most of the world knew about this situation and watched and worried. But few know of an event over the Mediterranean on June 6th of this year [2002] that could have had a serious bearing on that outcome. U.S. early warning satellites detected a flash that indicated an energy release comparable to the Hiroshima burst. We see about 30 such bursts per year, but this one was one of the largest we have ever seen. The event was caused by the impact of a small asteroid, probably about 5–10 meters in diameter, on the earth's atmosphere. Had you been situated on a vessel directly underneath, the intensely bright flash would have been followed by a shock wave that would have rattled the entire ship, and possibly caused minor damage.

The event of this June received little or no notice as far as we can tell. However, if it had occurred at the same latitude just a few hours earlier, the result on human affairs might have been much worse. Imagine that the bright flash accompanied by a damaging shock wave had occurred over India or Pakistan. To our knowledge, neither of those nations have the sophisticated sensors that can determine the difference between a natural NEO impact and a nuclear detonation. The resulting panic in the nuclear-armed and hair-triggered opposing forces could have been the spark that ignited a nuclear horror we have avoided for over a half century.

I've just relayed one aspect of NEOs that should worry us all. As more and more nations acquire nuclear weapons—nations without the sophisticated controls and capabilities built up by the United States over the 40 years of Cold War—we should ensure the 30-odd yearly impacts on the upper atmosphere are well understood by all to be just what they are.

A few years ago those of us charged with protecting this Nation's vital space systems, such as the Global Positioning System, became aware of another aspect of the NEO problem. This was the Leonid meteor storm. This particular storm occurs every 33 years. It is caused by the debris from a different type of NEO—a comet. When the earth passes through the path of a comet, it can encounter the dust thrown off by that comet through its progressive passes by the sun. This dust is visible on the earth as a spectacular meteor storm. But our satellites in space can experience the storm as a series of intensely damaging micrometeorite strikes. We know about many of these storms and we have figured out their parent comet sources. But there are some storms arising from comets that are too dim for us to see that can produce "surprise" events. One of these meteor storms has the potential of knocking out some or even most of our earth-orbiting systems. If just one random satellite failure in a pager communications satellite a few years ago seriously disrupted our lives, imagine what losing dozens of satellites could do.

> *I advocate we focus our energies on the smaller, more immediate threats.*

Most people know of the Tunguska NEO strike in Siberia in 1908. An object probably less than 100 meters in diameter struck Siberia, releasing equivalent energy of up to 10 megatons. Many experts believe there were two other smaller events later in the century—one in Central Asia in the 1940s and one in the Amazon in the 1930s. In 1996, our satellite sensors detected a burst over Greenland of approximately 100 kiloton yield. Had any of these struck over a populated area, thousands and perhaps hundreds of thousands might have perished. Experts now tell us that an even worse catastrophe than a land impact of a Tunguska-size event would be an ocean impact near a heavily populated shore. The resulting tidal wave could inundate shorelines for hundreds of miles and potentially kill millions. There are hundreds of thousands of objects the size of the Tunguska NEO that come near the earth. We know the orbits of just a few.

> **"** *New technologies for space-based and ground-based surveys of the entire space near the earth are available.* **"**

Finally, just about everyone knows of the "dinosaur killer" asteroids. These are objects, a few kilometers across, that strike on time scales of tens of millions of years. While the prospect of such strikes grabs people's attention and make great catastrophe movies, too much focus on these events has, in my opinion, been counterproductive. Most leaders in the United States or elsewhere believe there are more pressing problems than something that may only happen every 50–100 million years. I advocate we focus our energies on the smaller, more immediate threats. This is not to say we do not worry about the large threats. However, I'm reasonably confident we will find almost all large objects within a decade or less. If we find any that seem to be on a near-term collision course—which I believe unlikely—we can deal with the problem then.

What Should We Do?

First and foremost, when an object strikes the earth, we must know exactly what it is and where it hit. Fortunately, our early warning satellites already do a good job of this task. Our next generation system, the Space-Based Infrared System, will be even better. The primary difficulty is that this data is also used for vital early warning purposes and its detailed performance is classified. However, in recent years, the U.S. DoD has been working to provide extracts of this data to nations potentially under missile attack with cooperative programs known as "Shared Early Warning." Some data about asteroid strikes have also been released to the scientific community. Unfortunately, it takes several weeks for this data to be released. I believe we should work to assess and release this data as soon as possible to all interested parties, while ensuring sensitive performance data is safeguarded.

We have studied what a NEO warning center might look like. I believe adding a modest number of people, probably less than 10, to current early warning centers and supporting staffs within Cheyenne Mountain could form the basis of a Natural Impact Warning Clearinghouse.

Perhaps the most urgent mid-term task has already begun. This is the systematic observation and cataloging of nearly all potentially threatening NEOs. We are probably about halfway through cataloging "large" NEOs (greater than a kilometer in diameter). It is interesting to note the most effective sensor has been the MIT Lincoln Lab LINEAR facility in New Mexico, which is a test bed for the next generation of military ground-based space surveillance sensors. But this ground-based system, however effective, can only address the "large," highly unlikely threats. We find out every few weeks about "modest" asteroids a few hundred meters in diameter. Most sail by the earth unnoticed until they have passed. In recent months, the object 2002MN had just this sort of near miss–passing only a few tens of thousands of kilometers from the earth. Ground-based systems such as LINEAR are unable to detect one of the most potentially damaging classes of objects, such as comets that come at us from the direction of the sun. New space-surveillance systems capable of scanning the entire sky every few days are what is needed.

Technologies

New technologies for space-based and ground-based surveys of the entire space near the earth are available. These technologies could enable us to completely catalog and warn of objects as small as the Tunguska meteor (less than 100 meters in diameter). The LINEAR system is limited primarily by the size of its main optics—about one meter in diameter. By building a set of three-meter diameter telescopes equipped with new large-format Charged Coupled Devices, the entire sky could be scanned every few weeks and the follow-up observations necessary to accurately define orbits, particularly for small objects, could be done.

The most promising systems for wide-area survey—particularly to observe close to the sun to see objects coming up from that direction—are space-based surveillance systems. Today the only space-based space surveillance system is the DoD's Mid-course Space Experiment (MSX) satellite. This was a late 1990s missile defense test satellite, and most of its sensors have now failed. However, one small package weighing about 20 kg and called the Space-Based Visible sensor is able to search and track satellites in geosynchronous orbit (GEO) using visible light. This has been a phenomenally successful mission, having lowered the number of "lost" objects in GEO orbit by over a factor of two. MSX is not used for imaging asteroids, but a similar sensor could be. The Canadian Space Agency, in concert with the Canadian Department of National Defense, is considering a "microsatellite" experiment with the entire satellite and payload weighing just 60 kg. This Near-Earth Surveillance System would track satellites in GEO orbit, as MSX does today. However, it would also be able to search the critical region near the sun for NEOs that would be missed by conventional surveys.

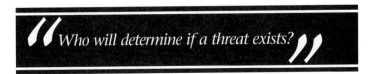

Who will determine if a threat exists?

The U.S. DoD is planning a constellation of somewhat larger satellites to perform our basic satellite-tracking mission. Today our ground-based radars and telescopes, and even MSX, only track objects that we already know about. These systems are not true outer-space search instruments as the LINEAR system is. However, the future military space surveillance system would be able to search the entire sky. As an almost "free" by-product, it could also perform the NEO search mission. Larger aperture ground-based systems could then be used to follow up to get accurate orbits for the NEOs discovered by the space-based search satellites. Again, I believe there is considerable synergy between national security requirements related to man-made satellites and global security requirements related to NEO impacts.

The Need for Research

Regardless of how well we know NEO orbits and can predict their impacts, the fact remains that today, we have insufficient information to contemplate mitigating an impact. We do not know the internal structure of these objects. Indeed, we have reason to believe that many, if not most, are more in the nature of "rubble piles" than coherent objects. This structure suggests that any effort to "push" or divert a NEO might simply fragment it, which could potentially turn a single dangerous asteroid into hundreds of objects that could damage a much larger area.

> *In my view, a single responsible nation would have the best chance of a successful NEO mitigation mission.*

What is needed are in situ measurements across the many classes of NEOs, including asteroids and comets. This is particularly important in the case of small (100 meter) class objects of the type we would most likely be called upon to divert. Until recently, missions to gather these data would have taken up to a decade to develop and launch and cost hundreds of millions of dollars. However, the situation looks much better with the emergence of so-called "microsatellites," which weigh between 50–200 kg and can be launched as almost "free" auxiliary payloads on large commercial and other flights to GEO orbit. These missions can be prepared in one to two years for about $5–10M, and launched for a few million dollars as an auxiliary payload. I believe such auxiliary accommodation is a standard feature on the European Ariane launches, and could be considered here in the United States on our new Evolved Expendable Launch Vehicles.

With a capable microsatellite with several kilometers per second "delta-V" (maneuver capacity) launched into a GEO transfer orbit (the standard initial launch orbit for placing systems into GEO), the satellite could easily reach some NEOs and perform in situ research. This could include sample return, direct impact to determine the internal structure and the potential to move a small object. Indeed, NASA is planning several small satellite missions. The key point here, however, is that with missions costing $10M each, we can sample many types of NEOs in the next decade or so to gain a full understanding of the type of objects we face.

There is an interesting concept to consider. If we can find

the right small object in the right orbit, we might be able to nudge it into an orbit "captured" by the earth. This would make a NEO a second natural satellite of earth. Indeed, there is at least one NEO that is close to being trapped by the earth now, 2002 AA29. If such an object were more permanently in earth orbit, it could be more closely studied and might form the basis for long-term commercial exploitation of space. Moreover, a very interesting manned space flight mission after the Space Station could be to an asteroid; maybe even one we put into earth's gravity sphere.

Command and Control

One important aspect of NEO mitigation is often overlooked. Host experts prefer to focus on the glamorous "mitigation" technologies—diverting or destroying objects. In fact, as the U.S. military knows well the harder part is what we call "command and control." Who will determine if a threat exists? Who will decide on the course of action? Who will direct the mission and determine when mission changes are to be made? Who will determine if the mission was successful? There are many more questions.

The U.S. military has long struggled with these command and control issues that now confront the NEO community. Earlier, I noted a concept of operations for the first step in NEO mitigation—Natural Impact Warning Clearinghouse. I believe this command and control operation could catalog and provide credible warning information on future NEO impact problems, as well as rapidly provide information on the nature of an impact.

International Issues

Many have suggested any NEO impact mitigation should be an international operation. In my opinion, the United States should proceed carefully in this area. International space programs, such as the International Space Station, fill many functions. A NEO mitigation program would have only one objective. In my view, a single responsible nation would have the best chance of a successful NEO mitigation mission. The responsible nation would not need to worry about giving up national security sensitive information and technology as it would build and control the entire mission itself. As I have pointed out, the means to identify threats and mitigate them overlap with other national security objectives.

> *NEO mitigation is a topic whose time has come.*

It does, however, make sense that the data gathered from surveys and in situ measurements be shared among all. This would maximize the possibility the nation best-positioned to perform a mitigation mission would come forward. One of the first tasks of the Natural Impact Warning Clearinghouse noted above could be to collect and provide a distribution point for such data.

Roles of the U.S. Military and NASA

Currently, NASA has been assigned the task of addressing some NEO issues. The U.S. DoD has been asked to assist this effort. However, the U.S. DoD has not been assigned tasks, nor has any item relating to NEOs been included in military operational requirements. I believe one option would be for the U.S. DoD to assume the role of collecting available data and assessing what, if any, threat might exist from possible NEO collisions of all sizes. This does not mean other groups, in particular the international scientific community, should not continue their independent efforts. However, the U.S. DoD is likely, for the foreseeable future, to have most of the required sensors to do this job. Moreover, in my view, the U.S. DoD has the discipline and continuity to ensure consistent, long-term focus for this important job. As a consequence of this function, the U.S. DoD might collect a large quantity of important scientific data. To the degree that the vast bulk of this has no military security implications, it could be released to the international scientific community.

In addition, I believe NASA should continue the scientific task of assessing the nature of NEOs. Performing the necessary scientific studies, including missions to NEOs to gather data, is among NASA's responsibilities. Like the 1994 U.S. DoD/NASA Clementine probe, these missions could serve as important technological demonstrations for the U.S. DoD, and might be conducted jointly with NASA.

Should a threatening NEO be discovered, it is my opinion the U.S. DoD could offer much toward mitigating the threat. Of course, with a funded and focused surveillance program for cataloging and scientific study as outlined above, we should have ample time to debate this issue before it becomes critical.

A Critical Issue

NEO mitigation is a topic whose time has come. I believe various aspects related to NEO impacts, including the possibility that an impact would be misidentified as a nuclear attack, are critical national and international security issues. The focus of NEO mitigation efforts—in finding and tracking them, and in exploring and moving some—should shift to smaller objects. The near-term threats are much more likely to come from these "small" objects (100 meters in diameter or so) and we might be able to divert such objects without recourse to nuclear devices.

After a suitable class of NEOs is found, microsatellite missions to explore and perhaps perform test divert operations could be considered. The technologies for low-cost NEO missions exist today.

The necessary command and control, sensor and space operations technologies and equipment are all "dual use" to the military. In my view, it stands to reason that strong military involvement should be considered in a national and international NEO program.

10

The Search for Extraterrestrial Life Is an Important Goal of Space Exploration

Seth Shostak

Seth Shostak is the public programs scientist at the SETI (Search for Extraterrestrial Intelligence) Institute in California. His research has included radio astronomy, dynamics of galaxies, image processing, and missing matter. He is the author of the book Sharing the Universe.

There is reason to believe that a first detection of a signal from an alien civilization could be coming soon. While it may prove challenging to decipher, the signal itself will be a message—a message that earthlings are not alone in the cosmos. Because it is overwhelmingly likely that the alien civilization will be far older than Earth's civilization, its technology will likely be considerably more advanced. Scientists will have the opportunity to potentially leapfrog thousands of years of research and accelerate Earth's sophistication and development.

On April 8 [2000] it will be exactly four decades since radio astronomer Frank Drake swung an antenna skyward hoping to find something other than the faint hiss of gas and galaxies. Drake was searching for a narrow-band whistle, a signal from a distant civilization.

His pioneering experiment used a small radio telescope in Green Bank, West Virginia. Since then, the search for extraterrestrial intelligence (SETI) has progressed to vastly improved equipment. Nonetheless, the dismaying fact is that none of the small coterie of scientists pursuing SETI have yet managed to find a single, confirmed chirp from the dark depths of the cosmos. The aliens, who I feel confident are out there, remain frustratingly out of sight.

But not out of mind. Today's SETI experiments are some 100 trillion times better than Drake's original search. In the next decade, new technologies and new telescopes will improve the capabilities for finding celestial societies by another factor of a thousand. While no one can be sure of success, many astronomers involved in these efforts, including me, suspect that we could soon have our first detection of an alien signal.

Preparing for Contact

If so, what happens next? Is humankind prepared to learn that the fictional aliens of Hollywood have living, unpredictable counterparts in the local galactic neighborhood? Would the news galvanize people with the excitement of a major discovery—or, alternatively, sound the alarms of fear?

It all depends. Our reaction hinges on the nature of the detection, the message (if any), and how the news is spread. Some of this is predictable, but much is not. So perhaps we shouldn't worry about it. After all, did fifteenth century Spaniards wring their hands over the possibility that Columbus might discover a new world, precipitating panic in the streets of Segovia? Hardly. More to the point: would the wringing of hands have helped?

In the case of SETI, some researchers believe it would. The reaction to a SETI detection *has* been considered. After all, SETI differs in a fundamental way from Columbus's voyage. The search is a deliberate investigation into the unknown. Discovery of a new world—an alien civilization—would not be an unforeseen by-product of SETI, but its primary intention. Consequently, sociologists, psychologists and others have produced a considerable body of literature describing what might happen and prescribing what should be done in case of success.

The SETI Declaration

In addition, the SETI researchers themselves have adopted an informal protocol that outlines actions to be taken by the discoverers. This protocol, *A Declaration of Principles Concerning Ac-*

tivities Following the Detection of Extraterrestrial Intelligence, assumes that our first tip-off of alien presence will be a radio (or optical) fingerprint: a signal from space.

> **//** *The aliens, who I feel confident are out there, remain frustratingly out of sight.* **//**

This is the type of search that I'm involved in. It is, of course, a direct descendant of Drake's 1960 experiment. My employer, the SETI Institute, is currently using the 1000-foot diameter Arecibo Radio Telescope in Puerto Rico to examine approximately a thousand nearby star systems for alien transmissions. This type of reconnaissance makes a lot of sense. It doesn't involve the assumption that the aliens are mounting a prodigious effort to get in touch. If a civilization 100 light years distant has an antenna the size of Arecibo, and beams a signal straight towards us, then a paltry 10 kilowatt transmitter will be sufficient to catch our attention.

Finding a signal may be our best hope for locating cosmic confreres. Anticipating this, the *Declaration* defines a series of steps that researchers should undertake to verify that the broadcast is truly extraterrestrial, and then it urges a rapid announcement to the astronomical community, to local governments and to the public. In other words, if our radio telescopes pick up ET, you'll quickly be reading about it in the papers. And because so many among the populace are convinced that aliens exist (even to the point of being blasé), there's little chance of rioting in the streets.

Cover-Up?

Mind you, some people, particularly in the United States (where belief in government conspiracy is considered a mark of political sophistication), are sure that a SETI detection would be hushed up rather than let loose on a labile public.

I am amused by this paranoia. Most SETI experiments, including all of the US efforts, are privately funded, and the government has no involvement. More to the point: there is no policy of secrecy within the research community, which means that—even as an interesting signal is being received—the scientists will be excitedly e-mailing friends and relatives.

I've seen this process in action on a few occasions, when our experiment has been briefly fooled by picking signals from space probes. These messages from robots that we've sent to the edge of the Solar System have many of the hallmarks we expect from an alien signal. While my colleagues and I were looking wild-eyed at the computers, I noted that the government showed no interest. The media, on the other hand, did.

> *Finding a signal may be our best hope for locating cosmic confreres.*

And even those who believe in a government conspiracy over UFOs could hardly claim the same for SETI. A signal from space is not something you can stack up in a secret hangar or hide behind six layers of barbed wire in the desert. A SETI signal can be easily confirmed and will be impossible to hide. There was a parallel in the seventeenth century. When clerics forced Galileo to desist from publishing his discoveries of Jupiter's large moons (a strong proof that the Earth was not the center of the Universe), he reputedly swallowed hard and muttered that "still, it moves." In other words, the evidence for his discovery was sitting in the sky awaiting confirmation by anyone with a cheap telescope and a few minutes' time. The same is true of a SETI signal: the word will be out, and fast.

Alien Hardware

Of course, it's also conceivable that we will find not a signal, but alien artifacts. Imagine that Hubble or some other large telescope accidentally captures an image of the exhaust radiation from an interstellar rocket. Or perhaps we will trip over colossal feats of astro-engineering involving the rearrangement of an alien society's entire planetary system. Such discoveries would undoubtedly be reported just as quickly as a SETI signal. The consequences, to my mind, would also be similar: a mammoth news story, inspiring follow-up research by just about every astronomer on the planet.

If the artifact were right on our doorstep, however, it would trigger a different response. We might—as suggested by Arthur C.

Clarke—discover a purpose-built monolith on the Moon. Another intriguing possibility is that we could find a time capsule at one of the Lagrangian points—gravitational dead spots in the Earth-Moon system where an alien memento could float in endless space storage. Perhaps we'll suddenly uncover an interstellar probe hanging out in our Solar System, or maybe the aliens will actually land at 10 Downing Street and demand satisfaction.

Such scenarios are entirely different (and, to my mind, enormously less probable) than the SETI success that I am considering here. They would provide physical evidence we could cart to the lab and—in the case of alien visitation—might confront us with a lethal threat. Some of the social researchers who consider what will happen if we find ET point to historical analogs such as Orson Welles's 1938 *War of the Worlds* radio broadcast, which panicked many people on the US East Coast. Such an apocalyptic reaction might follow a close encounter of the physical kind. But a microwave radio signal or a flashing infrared light beam, reaching us from hundreds or thousands of light-years away, is no reason to board the windows and head for the hills.

> *Of course, it's also conceivable that we will find not a signal, but alien artifacts.*

Instead, we'll slew all the telescopes we can in the direction of the incoming signal. Every observatory that can aim its instruments ET's way will do so. We'll quickly know something about the type of star system that houses this newly found society, as well as its distance. In addition, we can hope to measure slow shifts in the frequency of the incoming signal, caused by the Doppler effect as the transmitter moves. Assuming ET is broadcasting from a planetary surface, we'll be able to compute the length of the alien planet's day, and its year.

Message in a Radio Wave

All of this information will be exciting, yes, but what would really knock our hosiery off is to know what the aliens are saying. That requires additional work beyond detection. To make them more sensitive, the SETI receivers add up the incoming radio waves over fixed period—the time constant—which is typically a second or so. As a result, any variations in the signal that are faster than once per second are smoothed out and lost. A terrestrial TV signal, for example, varies about five million times per second, so if your home set were to have a one-second time constant, you'd find the telly a bore (or perhaps I should say, more of a bore). The screen would be a slowly changing, gray wash of light.

> *Since it's overwhelmingly likely that any civilization we detect will be technologically far older than our own, the message would be of great interest.*

Simply shortening the receivers' time constant isn't the trick, however. That just weakens the signal and makes it noisier. What we need is to boost the signal first, so we can still detect it even with a shorter time constant. In practice, that means SETI researchers will have to build far larger telescopes than they have today—perhaps ten thousand times larger. That's currently a financial impossibility, but if an alien signal is detected I fully expect that the money will be found to construct this super-instrument.

Suppose it happens. Suppose that we have not only tuned in to ET's broadcast, but we are happily downloading the bits that constitute the message. These bits will be recorded and distributed for analysis. After years of work, either we will succeed in figuring them out, or we won't. It's probably realistic to assume that we will comprehend the aliens only if they are broadcasting deliberately, trying to communicate with other worlds. They could be engaged in altruistic efforts either to enlighten their neighbors or simply get in touch with young, technological societies such as our own. In that case they'll devise a message that can be decoded fairly straightforwardly.

Since it's overwhelmingly likely that any civilization we detect will be technologically far older than our own, the message would be of great interest. The aliens could allow us to short-circuit thousands of years of research into physics, astronomy, and chemistry, and tunnel our way into a far more sophisticated future. This could be compared to the rediscovery of classical science during the Renaissance, but would be of much greater magnitude. (Mind you, this windfall of knowledge will impose certain burdens. Scientists, for example, will suddenly be confronted with answers to research problems that have consumed their entire careers. These earthly scientists may not be entirely gratified to yield their chance for a Nobel Prize to the aliens!)

Such a sudden discovery of knowledge is possible, and it's an exciting thought. But it's also conceivable—and I personally think more probable—that the message will be difficult and perhaps impossible to decode. Imagine if the classical Greeks were given the bits belched out by a modern telecommunications satellite. The Greeks were not dumb, but they wouldn't get very far in understanding this torrent of information.

The same could well happen to us. Imagine everyone from professional cryptographers to amateurs with a flair for puzzles taking a crack at understanding the hieroglyphics from space. The aliens' message would become the equivalent of a Mayan Codex or the Dead Sea Scrolls. Centuries of human effort might be expended in an attempt to understand this cosmic riddle beamed our way from a society we can never meet. When the headlines of the initial discovery are only a distant memory, humankind might still be busying itself with the message.

The Signal *Is* the Message

Such thoughts are quite speculative—and they are also, in some sense, irrelevant. The detection of an alien civilization will certainly be the biggest news story of all time. And it will be a lasting story, both because researchers will continue searching for the message contained within the signal and because it will heighten the hunt for other signals. But to paraphrase Marshall McCluhan, the signal *is* the message. For a million years, humans have lived on this planet surrounded by a bubble of isolation. We have seen the Universe, like a vast and intricate construction, stretching billions of light-years in all directions. We have not, as yet, found any inhabitants.

But if SETI someday becomes a discovery, rather than an experiment, the bubble will burst, and we will suddenly share the cosmic stage with myriad others. It is hard to imagine a greater metamorphosis.

11

Funding for Space Exploration Should Be Redirected to Domestic and Global Problems

Katha Pollitt

Katha Pollitt is a columnist for the Nation, *a liberal weekly magazine, and author of numerous books and essays on pop culture and politics.*

Space exploration efforts proposed by the government's new space initiative would cost hundreds of billions of dollars over the next few decades. While space exploration is exciting to contemplate and discuss, it seems somewhat trivial in comparison to many of the problems America and the rest of the world face. Global warming, AIDS, famine, illiteracy, and energy shortages are just a few of the many challenges that humankind needs to overcome. By redirecting the effort, funding, and resources from space exploration into social problems, science could pursue more urgent challenges and improve the lives of many people.

A while back, in a column calling for more arts funding, I observed that a lot more people are interested in classical music, ballet, theater and museums than are interested in space exploration, so the NEA [National Endowment for the Arts] should get at least as much money as NASA. Who cares, I blithely asked, what color rocks Mars has? Lots of *Nation* readers, as it turned out, and a number of staffers too. I had no idea.

Katha Pollitt, "Lost in Space," *The Nation*, vol. 278, February 2, 2004, p. 9. Copyright © 2004 by The Nation Magazine/The Nation Company, Inc. Reproduced by permission.

81

Now that George W. Bush is proposing to establish a long-term base on the moon as early as 2015 and eventually to send humans to Mars, I won't repeat the mistake of assuming that everyone shares my lack of enthusiasm for astronautery and outer space. According to a somewhat confusing AP-Ipsos poll, 48 percent (disproportionately men, but you knew that) favor Bush's proposals for space exploration and 48 percent oppose it, although only 38 percent support sending people, which the proposal involves (57 percent prefer using robots). Fifty-five percent oppose it when given the option of spending the money on education and healthcare, and two-thirds of Democrats oppose it when it is identified as a "Bush Administration" plan. But let's not quibble—space is probably fascinating once you get into it, like Wagner or *The Lord of the Rings* or football. Someday, it might even be interesting to know if there was ever life on Mars—although it would also be interesting to know who put those statues on Easter Island, or why so often you can tell who's calling by the way the telephone rings.

> **"** *Space isn't going anywhere—we can always study it later. Earth, however, may be going down the tubes a lot faster than we imagine.* **"**

Life is full of mysteries, I'm trying to say, and space is such an expensive one! Estimates of Bush's proposals run into the hundreds of billions of dollars over the next several decades. If you care about the deficit, as conservatives claimed they did until Bush created a huge one through tax cuts for the rich, it's hard to justify. Even if the immediate amount turns out to be much smaller—Bush has proposed only $1 billion in new funding over the next five years, leaving the big bills for his successor—does it really makes sense to spend a significant sum to satisfy an idle curiosity when we can spend the money solving some other, equally daunting scientific challenge that would actually make people happier, healthier and better able to fulfill their capabilities in their brief time on earth? I'm all for boldly going forth and expressing the human spirit—why can't we do that by solving the enormous scientific and technological challenges posed by global warming? Because that would involve admitting that global warming is happening? and is caused by human activity? In the January 13 [2004] *New York Times* Science section, the front page that carried Kenneth Chang's article championing the idea of a moon base also carried an ominous article detailing rising temperatures in the Alaskan tundra, which is now frozen for only 100 days a year; thirty years ago it was 200. Of the photographs in that section, which ones represent a phenomenon that is more likely to affect humanity first: the grim ones comparing the robust summer polar ice cap of 1979 with its moth-eaten 2003 self, or the lovely ones of planets and nebulae and galaxies illustrating the story on mapping the cosmos? Space isn't going anywhere—we can always study it later. Earth, however, may be going down the tubes a lot faster than we imagine. Those billions would fund a lot of environment-friendly innovation.

The Best Use of Science

As for science—fighting AIDS is science. "We can put a cowboy on Mars," quips my colleague Richard Kim, "or we can treat everyone on the planet with AIDS for the next generation. Three hundred billion dollars would pay for AIDS drugs at the generic prices cited in Bush's State of the Union address ($300 per year, per person) for all 40 million people with HIV for the next twenty-five years." Reproductive health is science. According to the January *Lancet*, half a million women die every year from pregnancy-related causes, 99 percent of them in underdeveloped countries; it's one of the most neglected health problems in the world today. Delivering quality care adapted to the circumstances of impoverished and often illiterate people living in isolated villages and farms, training a local healthcare force and paying it enough to stay put instead of fleeing to jobs in wealthier places, insuring women the human rights that undergird safe maternity, whether freedom from forced child marriage or access to family planning—that seems to me as urgent as setting up house on the moon.

Education is science—you could fund a lot of schools in poor countries, where 43 percent of boys and 48 percent of girls aren't even getting a primary education; you could buy a lot of books and maps and lab equipment and train a lot of teachers and create, in the next generation, a lot more scientists—let them go to the moon! We say we're so upset about the spread of Islamic fundamentalism—yet we stand by while rich Saudis set up Wahhabi madrassahs all over the Muslim world and invite poor parents to send their kids for free. These youngsters could be learning astronomy instead of memorizing the Koran. We could put our Mars money where our mouth is.

I actually believe in science. I believe we are clever enough to think our way out of the problems we make for ourselves. We need to think big—on contraception, medicine, pollution, energy, food, water. Indeed, one of the worst aspects of the Bush Administration is its contempt for science. Thanks to Bush, creationist tracts are being sold in national parks—did you know that the Grand Canyon is only a few thousand years old, like the rest of the world? And faith healers like David Hager, who thinks Jesus will cure your PMS, sit on FDA [Food and Drug Administration] advisory panels. Bush policies disregard serious research—on the effectiveness of condoms to prevent HIV, on the ineffectiveness of abstinence-only sex education—and shun the promise of stem cell research, all in obedience to the crabbed sexual taboos of the right.

Besides, doesn't the moon belong to everyone, not just NASA, not just the United States? Must lovers and lonely people from Newfoundland to Bangladesh look up at night and think: There's the moon, round and silvery and full of Republicans?

12

Space Exploration Should Be Funded by the Private Sector

Steve Bonta

Steve Bonta is a contributing writer to the New American, *a conservative weekly magazine.*

The general public seems to accept the argument that the federal government and its tax dollars are the key to scientific progress. However, it is unconstitutional for the government to use tax dollars for scientific study that has no national security purpose. In the case of space exploration, the government has had some success but has wasted billions of dollars on unsuccessful missions and malfunctioning equipment. In the past, the most successful scientists developed their ideas with their own or other private funding sources. Benjamin Franklin, Thomas Edison, and the Wright brothers are examples of monumental advances in science from private enterprise. Modern space travel itself is attributable to Robert Goddard, who by 1914 had privately developed and secured patents for liquid fuel and a multistage rocket. If permitted, private enterprise might achieve comparable results in space exploration more efficiently and save taxpayer money in the process.

If the excitement over NASA's Spirit rover on Mars is any indication, many Americans seem to accept that federal taxpayer dollars and government oversight are indispensable to scientific progress. But once upon a time, America's most successful in-

Steve Bonta, "Final Frontier for Private Enterprise," *The New American*, vol. 20, February 9, 2004, p. 44. Copyright © 2004 by *The New American*. Reproduced by permission.

ventors and scientists conducted research using their own funds or with the help of grants from private donors. Benjamin Franklin's pathbreaking work on electricity, Alexander Graham Bell's telephone, Thomas Edison's numerous inventions, and the Wright brothers' airplanes are all examples of private enterprise fueling scientific and technological advancement.

Modern space travel, in fact, owes its existence to the talents of Robert H. Goddard, the original "rocket scientist" and another brilliant product of American private enterprise. Goddard began experimenting with rocketry while a student at Worcester Polytechnic Institute, and by 1914 had earned U.S. patents both for liquid rocket fuel and for a multi-stage rocket using solid fuel. Working primarily at his own expense and with the help of several grants from private institutions, Goddard over the next several decades literally invented modern rocket science. He was the first to develop and successfully launch a liquid fuel rocket, in March of 1926. Three years later, he became the first to launch a rocket with a scientific payload (a barometer and camera). In 1932, Goddard developed a gyroscopic control apparatus for rocket flight and first used vanes situated in the rocket blast for guidance. In 1937, Goddard launched for the first time a rocket with a motor pivoted on gimbals and under the influence of a gyroscopic control system.

It was only with the outbreak of World War II that the federal government finally recognized Goddard's talents. He offered his services to the U.S. Navy and successfully developed jet-assisted takeoff systems and rocket motors capable of variable thrust. He died in August 1945, just before the end of the war.

Robert Goddard's work for the federal government late in life underscores an important point: Washington's interest in science and exploration is and always will be mostly military. Scientific research and development for military ends are, after all, constitutionally legitimate, whatever their budgetary expediency. But the federal government is not constitutionally authorized to use taxpayer dollars to promote science for its own sake. In general, the feds have a poor track record in the domain of pure scientific research, wasting extravagant sums on boondoggles like the Superconducting Supercollider and the Hubble Space Telescope (which, it will be recalled, suffered from a flawed lens and required an expensive manned space mission, years after the original launch, to repair it).

Because space has been militarized to a certain extent, further research and development into space-based military systems seems inevitable. But trips to the moon, Mars and elsewhere in the solar system have no foreseeable military application. The primary purpose of such programs is to furnish a regimentary national "sense of purpose" while squandering taxpayer monies. As President Kennedy famously put it, in a speech at Rice University in September 1962, "we choose to go to the moon in this decade and do . . . other things, not because they are easy, but because they are hard, because that goal will serve to organize and measure the best of our energies and skills." President Bush, in his recent announcement of an ambitious new program to resume missions to the moon and to prepare for an eventual manned mission to Mars, indicated that "we choose to explore space because doing so improves our lives, and lifts our national spirit."

The unspoken premise of statements like these is that only through strong, centralized political leadership and the use of federal taxpayer dollars can significant progress be made. Omitted is any acknowledgement that, if permitted, private enterprise might achieve comparable advances in space exploration with greater efficiency and at no cost to the taxpaying public.

While it is true that some government science projects, such as satellite development, have yielded unlooked-for bonanzas to the private sector, much of the space program has been a colossal waste of public funds because, compared with private enterprise, few incentives exist in the public sector for thrift, careful planning, ingenuity and sound decision-making. What is the value of admittedly mind-blowing photographs of distant nebulae and galaxy clusters when weighed against the literally astronomical sums of money spent on maintaining a leaky space station, an antiquated and unreliable shuttle fleet, and a never-ending stream of hit-or-miss space probes?

The romantic in all of us enjoys contemplating the limitless marvels of creation revealed in high-resolution photos of alien worlds and distant star systems. There can be little doubt that modern science is one of the triumphs of Western Civilization. But science itself, as the achievements of Robert Goddard and many other American scientific pioneers bear witness, is best carried out in the private sector, where the limitations of ever-fickle fiscal politics and dubious constitutionality are no hindrance to human creativity.

Organizations to Contact

The editors have compiled the following list of organizations concerned with the issues debated in this book. The descriptions are derived from materials provided by the organizations. All have publications or information available for interested readers. The list was compiled on the date of publication of the present volume; names, addresses, phone and fax numbers, and e-mail addresses may change. Be aware that many organizations take several weeks or longer to respond to inquiries, so allow as much time as possible.

Association of Space Explorers (ASE)
1150 Gemini Ave., Houston, TX 77058
(281) 280-8172 • fax: (281) 280-8173
Web site: www.space-explorers.org

The Association of Space Explorers, founded in 1985, is an international, nonprofit, professional, and educational organization of over three hundred individuals from twenty-nine nations who have flown in space. ASE's mission is to provide a forum for professional dialogue among individuals who have flown in space, support space science and exploration for the benefit of all, promote education in science and engineering, foster greater environmental awareness, and encourage international cooperation in the human exploration of space.

Center for Defense Information (CDI)
1779 Massachusetts Ave. NW, Washington, DC 20036
(202) 332-0600
Web site: www.cdi.org

The Center for Defense Information analyzes military spending, policies, and weapons systems. CDI opposes the deployment of space weapons.

Citizens for Peace in Space
PO Box 915, Colorado Springs, CO 80901
(719) 389-0644

This group, dedicated to the peaceful use of outer space, opposes all space weapons. It organizes protests at U.S. military bases that conduct space weapons research.

Global Network Against Weapons and Nuclear Power in Space (GN)
PO Box 652, Brunswick, ME 04011
(207) 729-0517 • (207) 319-2017
Web site: www.space4peace.org

The Global Network Against Weapons and Nuclear Power in Space was founded in 1992. At its yearly meetings, GN brings together key activists who are working on, or interested in, space issues. The founders' intention was to create a clearinghouse for space issues and ignite education and organizing in order to build an international citizens' movement.

National Aeronautics and Space Administration (NASA)
NASA Headquarters, Washington, DC 20546-0001
(202) 358-0000
Web site: www.nasa.gov

NASA is the federal agency in charge of the U.S. civil space program. It supports continued use of the space shuttle, construction of the International Space Station, and manned exploration of the moon and Mars. It also puts out many publications.

Planetary Society
65 North Catalina Ave., Pasadena, CA 91106-2301
(626) 793-5100 • fax: (626) 793-5528

The Planetary Society was founded in 1980 by Carl Sagan, Bruce Murray, and Louis Friedman to encourage the exploration of the solar system and the search for extraterrestrial life. The society is a nonprofit, nongovernmental organization, funded by dues and donations from individuals around the world. With more than one hundred thousand members from over 140 countries, it is the largest space interest group on earth.

SETI Institute
2035 Landings Dr., Mountain View, CA 94043
(650) 961-6633 • fax: (650) 961-7099
Web site: www.seti.org

The mission of the SETI (search for extraterrestrial intelligence) Institute is to explore, understand, and explain the origin, nature, and prevalence of life in the universe. The SETI Institute is a private, nonprofit organization dedicated to scientific research, education, and public outreach. Founded in 1984, the institute today employs more than a hundred scientists, educators, and support staff. Research at the institute is anchored by two centers, each directed by a renowned scientist who holds an endowed chair.

Space Studies Institute (SSI)
PO Box 82, Princeton, NJ 08542
(609) 921-0377
Web site: www.ssi.org

SSI is one of the leading research organizations for outer space colonization. Its research includes studies on lunar materials processing and alternative energy sources in space.

Students for the Exploration and Development of Space (SEDS)
MIT Room W20-445
77 Massachusetts Ave., Cambridge, MA 02139-4307
Web site: www.seds.org

SEDS is an independent, student-based organization that promotes the exploration and development of space. It pursues this mission by educating people about the benefits of space, supporting a network of interested students, providing an opportunity for members to develop their leadership skills, and inspiring people through its involvement in space-related projects.

U.S. Department of Defense (DOD)
Washington Headquarters Services
1155 Defense Pentagon, Washington, DC 20301
(703) 545-6700
Web site: www.defenselink.mil

The U.S. Department of Defense directs and controls all military operations and equipment in space through a series of agencies such as U.S. Space Command and the Missile Defense Agency.

Bibliography

Books

Paula Berinstein   *Making Space Happen: Private Space Ventures and the Visionaries Behind Them.* Medford, NJ: Medford, 2002.

Roger E. Bilstein   *Testing Aircraft, Exploring Space: An Illustrated History of NACA and NASA.* Baltimore: Johns Hopkins University Press, 2003.

Michael Cabbage   *Comm Check: The Final Flight of Shuttle Columbia.* New York: Free Press, 2004.

Tim Furniss   *A History of Space Exploration.* Guilford, CT: Lyons, 2003.

Karl Grossman   *Weapons in Space.* New York: Seven Stories, 2000.

Edward Hudgins   *Space: The Free Market Frontier.* Washington, DC: Cato Institute, 2002.

W. Henry Lambright   *Space Policy in the Twenty-First Century.* Baltimore: Johns Hopkins University Press, 2002.

Roger D. Launius and Howard E. McCurdy   *Imagining Space: Achievements, Predictions, Possibilities, 1950–2050.* San Francisco: Chronicle, 2001.

Howard E. McCurdy   *Faster, Better, Cheaper: Low-Cost Innovation in the U.S. Space Program.* Baltimore: Johns Hopkins University Press, 2003.

Alan E. Rubin   *Disturbing the Solar System.* Princeton, NJ: Princeton University Press, 2002.

Stephen Webb   *If the Universe Is Teeming with Aliens . . . Where Is Everybody?* New York: Copernicus, 2002.

Periodicals

Buzz Aldrin   "Just Doing Their Duty," *Los Angeles Times*, February 3, 2003.

Travis Charbeneau   "The Sky Is Falling," *Toward Freedom*, March/April 2001.

Tad Daley   "Our Mission on Mars," *Futurist*, September/October 2003.

Economist (U.S.)   "A Grand but Costly Vision," January 17, 2004.

Karen Auguston Field   "Why We Need a Mission to Mars," *Design News*, February 3, 2004.

Daren Fonda — "So You Want to Be an Astronaut?" *Time*, January 26, 2004.

Brace Gagnon — "Bush Launches a Dangerous Space Policy," *People's Weekly World*, January 17–23, 2004.

Ellen Goodman — "Missions Need a Greater Purpose," *Liberal Opinion Week*, February 17, 2003.

Jeff Jacoby — "Exploration of Space Won't End with Columbia," *Conservative Chronicle*, February 19, 2003.

Jeffrey Kluger — "Those Last Few Seconds," *Time*, March 24, 2003.

Paul Krugman — "A Failed Mission," *New York Times*, February 4, 2004.

David Masci — "NASA's Future," *CQ Researcher*, May 23, 2003.

Jon Mooallem — "Moonstruck," *Village Voice*, February 25–March 2, 2004.

New Scientist — "Bush's Final Frontier," January 24, 2004.

James Oberg — "The Rocky Road to Mars," *American Legion*, January 2001.

Eric Pianin — "Congressional Cold Feet," *Washington Post*, February 24, 2003.

Otis Port — "Space Travel: Bringing Costs Down to Earth," *Business Week*, February 2, 2004.

S. Fred Singer — "To the Moon of Mars; Saving the Bush Initiative," *Washington Times*, March 15, 2004.

Jeremi Suri — "New Age of Exploration," *Washington Times*, March 5, 2004.

John Noble Wilford — "Our Future in Space Is Already History," *New York Times*, February 9, 2003.

Index